MAD LIBS®

BEST OF MAD LIBS

By Roger Price and Leonard Stern

MAD LIBS

An Imprint of Penguin Random House LLC

Mad Libs format and text copyright © 2008, 2007, 2005, 2004, 2003, 2002, 2001, 2000, 1999,1998, 1997, 1996, 1995, 1994, 1993, 1990, 1989, 1988, 1985, 1982, 1979, 1976, 1970, 1968, 1965, 1959, 1958 by Penguin Random House LLC. First published in 2008 by Price Stern Sloan. All rights reserved.

Concept created by Roger Price & Leonard Stern

Published by Mad Libs,
an imprint of Penguin Random House LLC, New York.
Printed in the USA.

Visit us online at penguinrandomhouse.com

Best of Mad Libs ISBN 9780843126983
35 37 39 40 38 36 34

MAD LIBS is a registered trademark of Penguin Random House LLC.

MAD LIBS®
A ___MAD___ INTRODUCTION
ADJECTIVE

This fiftieth anniversary collection, *Best of Mad Libs*, is a testament to the enduring

fun of *Mad Libs*. In this book, *Mad Libs* cocreator Leonard Stern recounts how he

and his close friend Roger Price developed the word game that later became

Mad Libs. Plus, we've asked some celebrities to "fill in the blanks." Those who were

kind enough to participate include Steve Carell, Anne Hathaway, Henry Winkler,

Alan Arkin, and Aly & AJ. Best of all, we've included more than 125 of the funniest

Mad Libs stories that have been published during the past fifty years.

We hope this anniversary book makes you laugh out loud. After all, laughter is

the best _____.
　　　　　　　　　　NOUN

The creation of *Mad Libs* is directly linked to my inability to spell "hyperbole" in a seventh-grade spelling bee. Humiliated and embarrassed beyond words, I ran home to take refuge in the family dictionary, determined to learn the correct spelling and exact meaning of as many words as humanly possible. The dictionary became my constant companion—my roommate. Even today it's by my bedside, and on sleepless nights I make a point of learning at least one new word. Last night it was "orthogonal."

The first sighting of *Mad Libs* happened in 1953, and it remains indelibly etched in my mind. I was in my New York City apartment overlooking Central Park working on a Jackie Gleason *Honeymooners* script. Actually, I was sitting and staring at the typewriter (I still use one), searching for the precisely right adjective to describe the nose of Ralph Kramden's new boss. After wallowing in clichés for thirty minutes, I was ready to throw in the thesaurus when Roger Price (my best friend, fellow wordaholic, and the most original thinker I'd ever met, one of a kind of which there was no kind), showed up at my apartment. We had planned to do a final polish on our book, *What Not to Name the Baby*, based on Roger's bizarre theory that names exert more influence on our personalities than either heredity or environment. (Example: "Ashley" always looks like she's on her way to the dentist, and "Harry" always knows where to get more ice.) I apologized to Roger and told him we'd be cracking on the book in a moment. "No, we won't," he said. "You're in your idiosyncratic-pursuit-of-a-word mode. I could be standing here for hours. Do you want help?" Reluctant as I was to admit I did—I did. I said, "I need an adjective that—" and before I could further define my need, Roger said, "Clumsy and naked." I laughed out loud. Roger asked, "What's so funny?" I told him, thanks to his suggestions, Ralph Kramden now had a boss with a clumsy nose—or, if you will, a naked nose. Roger seldom laughed, but he did that time, confirming we were onto something—but what it was, we didn't know. "Clumsy" and "naked" were appropriately inappropriate adjectives that had led us to an incorrect but intriguing, slightly bizarre juxtaposing of words. Why? A *clumsy* nose indicated nature had failed or there had been a genetic mix-up, and an alliterative *naked* nose had the sound of a best-selling mystery novel. I remember thinking, *So what?* Then, suddenly and simultaneously, Roger and I realized what had happened. My obsession had produced an unpredictable wedding of words that had resulted in laughter—and a GAME! Abandoning Gleason and the book, we spent the rest of the day writing stories with key words left out. We played the game at a party that night. Hilarity reigned. Everyone thought this nameless game should be published. We agreed, but not until we came up with the right name. "Until" was five years later.

The name "Mad Libs" came to Roger and me out of the blue-plate special at Sardi's restaurant in New York in the summer of 1958. At the table next to us, an actor and his agent were having coffee and an argument. From what we couldn't help but overhear, the actor wanted to "ad-lib" an interview, and his agent thought it was a "mad" thing to do. 'Nuff said?

Abandoning our eggs Benedict, Roger and I were off and running to a publisher, the same one that had published Roger's best-selling humor book, *In One Head and Out the Other*. And within minutes we were in one door and out the other. Those good souls didn't think it was a book but honestly believed it might appeal to a game manufacturer. The game manufacturer in turn thought it was a book and sent us to another book publisher, which didn't think it was a book! After we ran out of publishers and game manufacturers within a fifty-mile radius of the city, Roger decided we should publish *Mad Libs* ourselves. What could it take? You design the book, find a printer, and place the order. So we did just that. It never occurred to us, until the printer called asking where he should deliver the books, that printers didn't double as warehouses. However, Roger's large Central Park West apartment could and did. Fourteen thousand copies of *Mad Libs* were delivered directly to his dining room, denying my good friend a decent sit-down meal for the three months and seventeen days it took us to find a willing, one-time-only distributor.

Once Roger and I knew that the books were in stores (we confirmed that by visiting bookstores), I arranged a meeting with Steve Allen. In 1958 I was head writer and comedy director for his top-rated Sunday night variety television show. Roger and I suggested to Steve we try *Mad Libs* as a way of introducing guest stars. Steve, a wordsmith himself, loved the idea of the audience supplying the missing words. We played *Mad Libs* on the show the very next Sunday to introduce our guest, Bob Hope. By Wednesday of the following week, the stores were sold out of *Mad Libs*. We needed another printing immediately. Roger held up the order until we could find a delivery destination other than his dining room.

In the early '60s, Larry Sloan, a dear friend from high school who had become successful as a journalist and publicist, and who had always been a grammarian *par excellence*, joined us as a partner and CEO, and we became the publishing company Price Stern Sloan. Before long, *PSS!* was the largest publisher on the West Coast, with *Mad Libs* having attained best-seller status.

About twenty years ago, I succumbed to personally promoting the company: I had MAD LIB printed on my California license plate. At red lights, with astonishing regularity, I was asked by the driver of the car next to me if I had anything to do with the word game *Mad Libs*. I would say, "Yes, I cocreated it." And they'd challengingly respond, "No way." Over time, it became increasingly apparent that no true Mad Libber believed that the game was of recent origin. I think in their heart of hearts they believed the game belonged to the past . . . that it had been around forever—from time immemorial. Eventually, I gave in. I now state emphatically that Moses had *Mad Libs* with him to keep the kids amused when they were on the road to Egypt. My red-light friends drive away happy.

When the sales of *Mad Libs* reached an astonishing one hundred million, I didn't walk, I ran to Roger's office to tell him the great news. Roger didn't speak at first, but when he did he issued a Rogerism that I have quoted continuously over the years. "Well," he said, "you can fool some of the people some of the time—and that's enough."

—Leonard Stern

INSTRUCTIONS

MAD LIBS® is a game for people who don't like games!
It can be played by one, two, three, four, or forty.

• RIDICULOUSLY SIMPLE DIRECTIONS

In this tablet you will find stories containing blank spaces where words are
left out. One player, the READER, selects one of these stories. The READER
does not tell anyone what the story is about. Instead, he/she asks the other
players, the WRITERS, to give him/her words. These words are used to fill
in the blank spaces in the story.

• TO PLAY

The READER asks each WRITER in turn to call out a word—an adjective
or a noun or whatever the space calls for—and uses them to fill in the
blank spaces in the story. The result is a MAD LIBS® game.

When the READER then reads the completed MAD LIBS® game to the
other players, they will discover that they have written a story that is
fantastic, screamingly funny, shocking, silly, crazy, or just plain dumb—
depending upon which words each WRITER called out.

• EXAMPLE (*Before* and *After*)

"_____!" he said _____
        EXCLAMATION   ADVERB

as he jumped into his convertible _____ and
                                              NOUN

drove off with his _____ wife.
                            ADJECTIVE

"_____*Ouch*_____!" he said _____*stupidly*_____
        EXCLAMATION   ADVERB

as he jumped into his convertible _____*cat*_____ and
                                              NOUN

drove off with his _____*brave*_____ wife.
                            ADJECTIVE

MAD LIBS®
QUICK REVIEW

In case you have forgotten what adjectives, adverbs, nouns, and verbs are, here is a quick review:

An ADJECTIVE describes something or somebody. *Lumpy, soft, ugly, messy,* and *short* are adjectives.

An ADVERB tells how something is done. It modifies a verb and usually ends in "ly." *Modestly, stupidly, greedily,* and *carefully* are adverbs.

A NOUN is the name of a person, place, or thing. *Sidewalk, umbrella, bridle, bathtub,* and *nose* are nouns.

A VERB is an action word. *Run, pitch, jump,* and *swim* are verbs. Put the verbs in past tense if the directions say PAST TENSE. *Ran, pitched, jumped,* and *swam* are verbs in the past tense.

When we ask for A PLACE, we mean any sort of place: a country or city *(Spain, Cleveland)* or a room *(bathroom, kitchen)*.

An EXCLAMATION or SILLY WORD is any sort of funny sound, gasp, grunt, or outcry, like *Wow!, Ouch!, Whomp!, Ick!,* and *Gadzooks!*

When we ask for specific words, like a NUMBER, a COLOR, an ANIMAL, or a PART OF THE BODY, we mean a word that is one of those things, like *seven, blue, horse,* or *head*.

When we ask for a PLURAL, it means more than one. For example, *cat* pluralized is *cats*.

A BIOGRAPHY OF STEVE CARELL

ADJECTIVE _bloated_

PLURAL NOUN _hardwood floors_

NOUN _reduced-fat Oreo_

ADJECTIVE _slightly-impaired_

ADJECTIVE _evil_

NOUN _toupee_

VERB ENDING IN "ING" _sashaying_

VERB (PAST TENSE) _acquitted_

ADJECTIVE _really fun_

ADJECTIVE _homeschooled_

NOUN _electric razor_

NOUN _Shriner's parade_

NOUN _estrogen_

NOUN _window treatment_

PLURAL NOUN _wide-wale corduroys_

ADJECTIVE _freshly-baked_

PERSON IN ROOM _Johnny_

NOUN _sponge_

PART OF THE BODY _lap_

ADJECTIVE _flourescent_

NOUN _bruschetta_

Celebrities were asked to give answers to these parts of speech without seeing the stories on the next page.

MAD LIBS®

A BIOGRAPHY OF STEVE CARELL

Today, Steve Carell's __bloated__ face is known to millions of television
ADJECTIVE

and movie __hardwood floors__ all over the __reduced-fat Oreo__. But,
PLURAL NOUN   NOUN

as is often the case, it took years of really __slightly-impaired__ work for
ADJECTIVE

this __evil__ actor to become an overnight __toupee__. After more than two
ADJECTIVE   NOUN

decades of __sashaying__ in improv theater, Steve __acquitted__ it big
VERB ENDING IN "ING"   VERB (PAST TENSE)

as a faux newsman on *The Daily Show with Jon Stewart*. This success led to

an attention-grabbing role in the __really fun__ blockbuster, *Bruce*
ADJECTIVE

__homeschooled__. Practically overnight, Steve became a household
ADJECTIVE

__electric razor__ in television and film. He won a Golden
NOUN

__Shriner's parade__ Award for television's *The Office*. In his first starring
NOUN

__estrogen__, *The 40-Year-Old* __Window treatment__, which he cowrote,
NOUN   NOUN

he received critical acclaim and broke box office __wide-wale corduroys__.
PLURAL NOUN

More recently, he starred in the __freshly-baked__ comedy hit, __Johnny__
ADJECTIVE   PERSON IN ROOM

Almighty, and in June 2008, he's playing Maxwell Smart in the big-screen

version of '60s TV series, *Get* __sponge__. According to close friends,
NOUN

"Success has not gone to Steve's __lap__." They all say he "remains the
PART OF THE BODY

same __flourescent__ __bruschetta__ he's always been."
ADJECTIVE   NOUN

Celebrities were asked to give answers to the parts of speech on the previous page without seeing the stories above.

A Biography of Anne Hathaway

NOUN ___police officer___

VERB ___sneeze___

PART OF THE BODY ___nostril___

NOUN ___foyer___

PLURAL NOUN ___ice skates___

ADJECTIVE ___moist___

PLURAL NOUN ___frappuccinos___

NOUN ___arena___

NOUN ___crow___

VERB ENDING IN "ING" ___hearing___

NOUN ___risotto___

ADJECTIVE ___motley___

NOUN ___kangaroo___

PART OF THE BODY ___patella___

PLURAL NOUN ___satchels___

VERB ENDING IN "ING" ___breaching___

NOUN ___riding crop___

MAD LIBS®

A Biography of Anne Hathaway

Anne Hathaway's career has taken off like a rocket to the __police officer__.
NOUN

The daughter of an actress, Anne was inspired to __sneeze__ in her
VERB

mother's __nostril__-steps. Her breakthrough __foyer__, *The*
PART OF THE BODY   NOUN

Princess __ice skates__, established Anne as a/an __moist__
PLURAL NOUN   ADJECTIVE

actress with impeccable comic __frappuccinos__. This ability to be funny
PLURAL NOUN

served her well, as Meryl Streep's co-__arena__ in *The Devil Wears*
NOUN

__crow__. Anne proved herself equally at home in a dramatic role
NOUN

in the Academy Award-__hearing__ *Brokeback* __risotto__.
VERB ENDING IN "ING"   NOUN

In June 2008, Anne graces the screen once more, happily recreating the role of

Agent 99 in the film version of *Get* __motley__. When Anne is not in
ADJECTIVE

front of the __kangaroo__, she relaxes by burying her __patella__
NOUN   PART OF THE BODY

in nonfiction __satchels__, __breaching__ the piano, and, as a
PLURAL NOUN   VERB ENDING IN "ING"

trained singer, bursting into an operatic __riding crop__ when the mood
NOUN

strikes her.

A BIOGRAPHY OF ALAN ARKIN

NOUN ___HONORÉ DE BALZAC___

ADJECTIVE ___SQUEAMISH___

NOUN ___GENERAL SCHWARZKOPF___

NOUN ___SERGEANT YORK___

VERB (PAST TENSE) ___SQUATTED___

NOUN ___SPARTACUS___

PERSON IN ROOM ___ALBERT SCHWEITZER___

VERB ___STUMBLE___

NOUN ___ZEUS___

ADJECTIVE ___SLEAZY___

PLURAL NOUN ___VIENNA BOYS CHOIRS___

VERB ENDING IN "ING" ___PRIMPING___

ADJECTIVE ___OILY___

NOUN ___BUCKET___

NOUN ___TWEEZER___

NOUN ___OLIVE OIL___

NOUN ___KLEENEX___

NOUN ___FIG TREE___

ADJECTIVE ___GARISH___

Celebrities were asked to give answers to these parts of speech without seeing the stories on the next page.

MAD LIBS®
A BIOGRAPHY OF ALAN ARKIN

Alan Arkin first saw the light of <u>HONORÉ DE BALZAC</u> in Brooklyn, New York.
NOUN

As a struggling <u>SQUEAMISH</u> actor and a wannabe guitarist/songwriter, he
ADJECTIVE

played bit parts on television and stage, but essentially made his living as a/an

<u>GENERAL SCHWARZKOPF</u>-washer in a restaurant. Occasionally, he booked a
NOUN

gig playing his <u>SERGEANT YORK</u> and singing songs he <u>SQUATTED</u>.
NOUN   VERB (PAST TENSE)

In 1956, Arkin cowrote the Jamaican calypso "Banana Boat Song," also known

as "Day-o," which became a blockbuster <u>SPARTACUS</u>. In 1963, Alan caught
NOUN

the eye of <u>ALBERT SCHWEITZER</u>, a casting agent, and was signed to
PERSON IN ROOM

<u>STUMBLE</u> in the Broadway play, *Enter Laughing*, for which he won the
VERB

prestigious Tony <u>ZEUS</u>. His movie career has been one <u>SLEAZY</u>
NOUN   ADJECTIVE

success after another. In his debut film, *The <u>VIENNA BOYS CHOIRS</u> Are*
PLURAL NOUN

Coming, The Russians Are <u>PRIMPING</u>, he earned his first Academy Award
VERB ENDING IN "ING"

nomination, and he received another for his <u>OILY</u> performance in *The*
ADJECTIVE

Heart Is a Lonely <u>BUCKET</u>. *Little Miss <u>TWEEZER</u>-shine* brought him
NOUN   NOUN

his third nomination and his first Academy <u>OLIVE OIL</u> as Best Supporting
NOUN

<u>KLEENEX</u>. And in June 2008, Alan lends his distinctive acting <u>FIG TREE</u>
NOUN   NOUN

to the role of the chief of Control in the movie, *Get <u>GARISH</u>*.
ADJECTIVE

A Biography of Henry Winkler

ADJECTIVE ___ridiculous___

PLURAL NOUN ___trout___

ADJECTIVE ___mushy___

ADJECTIVE ___boisterous___

ADJECTIVE ___infectious___

PLURAL NOUN ___roses___

NOUN ___Linus___

NOUN ___birdbath___

PLURAL NOUN ___weed wackers___

NOUN ___applesauce___

PLURAL NOUN ___belly buttons___

VERB ENDING IN "ING" ___sleeping___

NOUN ___Swiss Army Knife___

ADJECTIVE ___stinky___

PLURAL NOUN ___rubber bands___

NOUN ___boot___

PLURAL NOUN ___mouse ears___

VERB ___stroke___

PERSON IN ROOM ___Hank Zipzer___

PLURAL NOUN ___lawn mowers___

As is true of most ___ridiculous___ actors, Henry Winkler started out by doing
ADJECTIVE

one-line ___trout___ and ___mushy___ commercials. But once he landed
PLURAL NOUN   ADJECTIVE

the ___boisterous___ role of "The Fonz" in the ___infectious___ sitcom,
ADJECTIVE   ADJECTIVE

Happy ___roses___, he was on his way to becoming an overnight
PLURAL NOUN

___Linus___. This Yale graduate's portrayal of high school dropout
NOUN

Arthur Fonzarelli earned him two Golden ___birdbath___ Awards, three
NOUN

Emmy ___weed wackers___, and made him the ___applesauce___-age idol
PLURAL NOUN   NOUN

of the seventies. Constantly in demand, Henry worked steadily in feature

___belly buttons___ and many guest ___sleeping___ roles in television,
PLURAL NOUN   VERB ENDING IN "ING"

until he sought refuge behind the camera as a director, producer, and

___Swiss Army Knife___. His deep commitment to children's welfare led
NOUN

him to coauthor a/an ___stinky___ series of kids' books about a character
ADJECTIVE

named Hank Zipzer which made *The New York* ___rubber bands___ best-seller
PLURAL NOUN

___boot___ and received critically acclaimed ___mouse ears___. If you
NOUN   PLURAL NOUN

ask Henry what he's proudest of he will quickly ___stroke___, "Writing the
VERB

___Hank Zipzer___ ___lawn mowers___ with my partner Lin Oliver."
PERSON IN ROOM   PLURAL NOUN

Q & A with AJ Michalka of Aly & AJ

NUMBER ___8___

ADJECTIVE ___gritty___

NOUN ___grandma___

PART OF THE BODY ___belly button___

ADJECTIVE ___salty___

VERB ENDING IN "ING" ___flying___

PLURAL NOUN ___cars___

PLURAL NOUN ___spoons___

PART OF THE BODY (PLURAL) ___ears___

NOUN ___sofa___

NOUN ___loser___

NOUN ___leprechaun___

ADJECTIVE ___lazy___

PLURAL NOUN ___dolphin___

PLURAL NOUN ___babes___

NOUN ___dude___

ADJECTIVE ___fuzzy___

MAD LIBS®

Q & A with AJ Michalka of Aly & AJ

Q: For someone who has yet to turn _____**8**_____-years-old, you've had a/an
NUMBER

_____**gritty**_____ career. How did you get started?
ADJECTIVE

A: Modeling! I was a professional _____**grandma**_____ and a very lucky one. My
NOUN

_____**belly button**_____ was on the cover of many _____**salty**_____ magazines.
PART OF THE BODY   ADJECTIVE

Q: You've been _____**flying**_____ steadily as an actress in television and
VERB ENDING IN "ING"

_____**cars**_____. Of all the _____**spoons**_____ you've worked on, which was your favorite?
PLURAL NOUN   PLURAL NOUN

A: It was cool working on Six _____**ears**_____ Under. And having a
PART OF THE BODY (PLURAL)

recurring _____**sofa**_____ in the _____**loser**_____ opera, General _____**leprechaun**_____,
NOUN   NOUN   NOUN

was a really _____**lazy**_____ experience.
ADJECTIVE

Q: You have an upbeat personality. Do you ever get down in the _____**dolphins**_____?
PLURAL NOUN

A: Mom wouldn't allow that. Remember, she was a cheerleader for the Oakland

_____**babes**_____.
PLURAL NOUN

Q: In the last three years, you and Aly have been turning out one hit

_____**dude**_____ after another. Do you ever have time for your hobbies?
NOUN

A: I make time. I enjoy reading, and I also love hanging out with my

_____**fuzzy**_____ family.
ADJECTIVE

Q & A with Aly Michalka of Aly & AJ

PLURAL NOUN — _gnomes_

PART OF THE BODY — _pinkie toe_

NOUN — _garbage truck_

ADJECTIVE — _gnarly_

PLURAL NOUN — _text messages_

PART OF THE BODY (PLURAL) — _earlobes_

NOUN — _lightbulb_

NOUN — _boyfriend_

ADJECTIVE — _eccentric_

PLURAL NOUN — _footballs_

PART OF THE BODY — _booty_

PART OF THE BODY — _kidney_

PLURAL NOUN — _chicken pot pies_

PART OF THE BODY (PLURAL) — _nostrils_

MAD LIBS®

MAD LIBS®

Q & A with Aly Michalka of Aly & AJ

Q: I'm sure you've heard this before, but you and AJ are spitting __gnomes__
PLURAL NOUN

of each other. You look alike, but do you think alike?

A: We get along well, but there are times we don't see eye to __pinkie toe__.
PART OF THE BODY

Q: Your debut album, *Into the* __garbage truck__, was a/an __gnarly__
NOUN   ADJECTIVE

success. Did you anticipate it would go right to the top of the charts and sell more

than a million __text messages__?
PLURAL NOUN

A: We kept our __earlobes__ crossed.
PART OF THE BODY (PLURAL)

Q: On your latest album, *Insomniatic*, you willingly and musically went out on a

__lightbulb__ to introduce a brand-new __boyfriend__. Why take
NOUN   NOUN

the risk?

A: We had an overwhelming urge to create a/an __eccentric__ sound that
ADJECTIVE

would allow us to inspirationally express our heartfelt __footballs__.
PLURAL NOUN

Q: Well, you certainly succeeded. It's apparent to anyone who listens to

Insomniatic that the songs come from your __booty__, and it's obvious
PART OF THE BODY

that success hasn't gone to your __kidney__, either.
PART OF THE BODY

A: We owe it all to our parents. They are great role __chicken pot pies__.
PLURAL NOUN

They keep our __nostrils__ planted firmly on the ground.
PART OF THE BODY (PLURAL)

Celebrities were asked to give answers to the parts of speech on the previous page without seeing the stories above.

MAD LIBS® is fun to play with friends, but you can also play it by yourself! To begin with, DO NOT look at the story on the page below. Fill in the blanks on this page with the words called for. Then, using the words you have selected, fill in the blank spaces in the story.

Now you've created your own hilarious MAD LIBS® game!

LITTLE RED RIDING HOOD

COLOR _____

PLURAL NOUN _____

ADJECTIVE _____

EXCLAMATION _____

SILLY WORD _____

VERB (PAST TENSE) _____

PLURAL NOUN _____

VERB _____

PLURAL NOUN _____

VERB _____

PLURAL NOUN _____

MAD LIBS®
LITTLE RED RIDING HOOD

One day, Little _____ Riding Hood was going through the forest
                     COLOR

carrying a basket of _____ for her grandmother. Suddenly,
                          PLURAL NOUN

she met a big _____ wolf. "_____!" said the
                   ADJECTIVE   EXCLAMATION

wolf. "Where are you going, little _____?" "I'm going to my
                                      SILLY WORD

grandmother's house," she said. Then the wolf _____
                                                  VERB (PAST TENSE)

away. When Miss Riding Hood got to her grandmother's house, the wolf was

in bed dressed like her grandmother. "My, Grandmother," she said. "What big

_____ you have." "The better to _____ you with,"
  PLURAL NOUN   VERB

said the wolf. "And, Grandmother," she said, "what big _____
                                                           PLURAL NOUN

you have." The wolf said, "The better to _____ you with." And
                                             VERB

then she said, "What big _____ you have, Grandmother." But the
                            PLURAL NOUN

wolf said nothing. He had just died of indigestion from eating Grandmother.

MAD LIBS® is fun to play with friends, but you can also play it by yourself! To begin with, DO NOT look at the story on the page below. Fill in the blanks on this page with the words called for. Then, using the words you have selected, fill in the blank spaces in the story.

Now you've created your own hilarious MAD LIBS® game!

TALK LIKE A PIRATE

NOUN _____

ADJECTIVE _____

VERB _____

ADVERB _____

NOUN _____

ADJECTIVE _____

PLURAL NOUN _____

PLURAL NOUN _____

PLURAL NOUN _____

PART OF THE BODY _____

NOUN _____

NOUN _____

NOUN _____

NOUN _____

PART OF THE BODY _____

MAD LIBS®

TALK LIKE A PIRATE

Ye can always pretend to be a bloodthirsty _____, threatening
NOUN

everyone by waving yer _____ sword in the air, but until ye learn
ADJECTIVE

to _____ like a pirate, ye'll never be _____ accepted
VERB   ADVERB

as an authentic _____. So here's what ye do: Cleverly work into
NOUN

yer daily conversations _____ pirate phrases such as "Ahoy there,
ADJECTIVE

_____," "Avast, ye _____," and "Shiver me
PLURAL NOUN   PLURAL NOUN

_____." Remember to drop all yer *gs* when ye say such words as
PLURAL NOUN

sailin', *spittin'*, and *fightin'*. This will give ye a/an _____ start to
PART OF THE BODY

being recognized as a swashbucklin' _____. Once ye have the lingo
NOUN

down pat, it helps to wear a three-cornered _____ on yer head,
NOUN

stash a/an _____ in yer pants, and keep a/an _____
NOUN   NOUN

perched atop yer _____. Aye, now ye be a real pirate!
PART OF THE BODY

MAD LIBS® is fun to play with friends, but you can also play it by yourself! To begin with, DO NOT look at the story on the page below. Fill in the blanks on this page with the words called for. Then, using the words you have selected, fill in the blank spaces in the story.

Now you've created your own hilarious MAD LIBS® game!

BEARS

ADJECTIVE _____

NOUN _____

PLURAL NOUN _____

ADJECTIVE _____

ADJECTIVE _____

VERB ENDING IN "ING" _____

VERB ENDING IN "ING" _____

ADJECTIVE _____

ADJECTIVE _____

NOUN _____

TYPE OF FOOD (PLURAL) _____

PART OF THE BODY (PLURAL) _____

ADJECTIVE _____

VEHICLE _____

TYPE OF FOOD (PLURAL) _____

TYPE OF FOOD (PLURAL) _____

SOMETHING ALIVE (PLURAL)_____

SOMETHING ALIVE (PLURAL)_____

ADVERB _____

NOUN _____

MAD LIBS®
BEARS

If you go to some _____ place like Yellowstone National _____,
                      ADJECTIVE   NOUN

you must know how to deal with wild animals such as bears and wolves

and _____. The most important of these is the bear. There are three
      PLURAL NOUN

kinds of bears at Yellowstone: the grizzly bear, the _____ bear, and
                                            ADJECTIVE

the _____ bear. Bears spend most of their time _____
     ADJECTIVE   VERB ENDING IN "ING"

or _____. They look very _____, but if you make
    VERB ENDING IN "ING"   ADJECTIVE

them _____, they might bite your _____. Bears will come
     ADJECTIVE   NOUN

up to your car and beg for _____. They will stand on their hind
                        TYPE OF FOOD (PLURAL)

legs and clap their _____ together and pretend to be
                      PART OF THE BODY (PLURAL)

_____. But do not get out of your _____ or offer
  ADJECTIVE   VEHICLE

the bears _____ or _____. This same advice
       TYPE OF FOOD (PLURAL)   TYPE OF FOOD (PLURAL)

applies to other wild creatures such as _____ and
                             SOMETHING ALIVE (PLURAL)

_____. Remember all these rules and you will spend your
SOMETHING ALIVE (PLURAL)

vacation _____ and not get eaten by a/an _____.
        ADVERB   NOUN

MAD LIBS® is fun to play with friends, but you can also play it by yourself! To begin with, DO NOT look at the story on the page below. Fill in the blanks on this page with the words called for. Then, using the words you have selected, fill in the blank spaces in the story.

Now you've created your own hilarious MAD LIBS® game!

PROMOS

FIRST NAME (MALE) _____

FIRST NAME (FEMALE) _____

NOUN _____

ARTICLE OF CLOTHING (PLURAL) _____

PART OF THE BODY _____

NOUN _____

PART OF THE BODY (PLURAL) _____

LAST NAME OF PERSON IN ROOM _____

ADJECTIVE _____

ADJECTIVE _____

PLURAL NOUN _____

NOUN _____

ADVERB _____

NOUN _____

ADVERB _____

ADJECTIVE _____

PLURAL NOUN _____

NOUN _____

MAD LIBS®
PROMOS

Newspaper critics agree that _____ and _____ are
                                 FIRST NAME (MALE)   FIRST NAME (FEMALE)

a comedy _____ that will knock your _____ off.
            NOUN   ARTICLE OF CLOTHING (PLURAL)

"It will tickle your funny _____!"
                             PART OF THE BODY

                              —The Washington _____
                                                      NOUN

"Two _____ up!"
       PART OF THE BODY (PLURAL)

                              —Ebert & _____
                                        LAST NAME OF PERSON IN ROOM

"A smart, _____, and _____ comedy. You
             ADJECTIVE   ADJECTIVE

not only laugh, but it brings _____ to your eyes."
                                 PLURAL NOUN

                      —The New Orleans Times-_____
                                                     NOUN

"A/An _____ funny half-hour _____; _____
           ADVERB   NOUN   ADVERB

acted by a/an _____ cast of all-star _____."
                 ADJECTIVE   PLURAL NOUN

                      —Chicago Sun-_____
                                         NOUN

MAD LIBS® is fun to play with friends, but you can also play it by yourself! To begin with, DO NOT look at the story on the page below. Fill in the blanks on this page with the words called for. Then, using the words you have selected, fill in the blank spaces in the story.

Now you've created your own hilarious MAD LIBS® game!

AFRAID OF THE DARK

PLURAL NOUN _____

VERB ENDING IN "ING" _____

NOUN _____

NOUN _____

PLURAL NOUN _____

PART OF THE BODY _____

NOUN _____

VERB ENDING IN "ING" _____

PART OF THE BODY (PLURAL) _____

VERB ENDING IN "ING" _____

NOUN _____

NOUN _____

PART OF THE BODY _____

ADVERB _____

PART OF THE BODY (PLURAL) _____

MAD LIBS®
AFRAID OF THE DARK

I was home alone and scared out of my _____. I could hear
                                        PLURAL NOUN

the wind _____, and off in the distance a/an _____
          VERB ENDING IN "ING"   NOUN

was howling. I crossed the room, locked the _____, and
                                              NOUN

climbed into bed, pulling the _____ over my _____.
                                PLURAL NOUN   PART OF THE BODY

Then it happened. I could hear a/an _____ _____
                                      NOUN   VERB ENDING IN "ING"

up the stairs. My _____ started to chatter and my knees
                   PART OF THE BODY (PLURAL)

began _____. The _____ was thrust
        VERB ENDING IN "ING"   NOUN

open and there was a huge _____ with hair all over his
                            NOUN

_____. It was my father. "Hi, we're home," he said _____.
PART OF THE BODY   ADVERB

"Hope you weren't afraid of staying home alone." "No," I said, lying through my

_____.
PART OF THE BODY (PLURAL)

MAD LIBS® is fun to play with friends, but you can also play it by yourself! To begin with, DO NOT look at the story on the page below. Fill in the blanks on this page with the words called for. Then, using the words you have selected, fill in the blank spaces in the story.

Now you've created your own hilarious MAD LIBS® game!

NEW YEAR'S RESOLUTIONS

PLURAL NOUN _____

NOUN _____

VERB _____

TYPE OF FOOD _____

PLURAL NOUN _____

PLURAL NOUN _____

ADJECTIVE _____

PLURAL NOUN _____

VERB _____

TYPE OF LIQUID _____

PART OF THE BODY (PLURAL) _____

ARTICLE OF CLOTHING (PLURAL) _____

ADJECTIVE _____

ADVERB _____

ADJECTIVE _____

MAD LIBS
NEW YEAR'S RESOLUTIONS

I resolve that in the next year I will eat all of my _____, just
                                                        PLURAL NOUN

like my mother says. I promise to help bathe my pet _____
                                                              NOUN

and help _____ the dishes after dinner.
             VERB

I will not eat any _____ that contains cholesterol or
                        TYPE OF FOOD

_____. I will be polite and thoughtful, and will clear the
        PLURAL NOUN

_____ after meals. I will do a/an _____
    PLURAL NOUN   ADJECTIVE

deed every day. I will be polite to any _____ who are older
                                              PLURAL NOUN

than I am. And I will never, ever _____ my dog's tail or pour
                                        VERB

_____ on my cat.
    TYPE OF LIQUID

I will also try to brush my _____ and shine my
                                  PART OF THE BODY (PLURAL)

_____ every day. I promise to be really _____
ARTICLE OF CLOTHING (PLURAL)   ADJECTIVE

so I can live _____ for the next twelve months. Then I'll be a
                    ADVERB

truly happy, _____ person.
                  ADJECTIVE

MAD LIBS® is fun to play with friends, but you can also play it by yourself! To begin with, DO NOT look at the story on the page below. Fill in the blanks on this page with the words called for. Then, using the words you have selected, fill in the blank spaces in the story.

Now you've created your own hilarious MAD LIBS® game!

CAMPFIRE STORIES

PLURAL NOUN _____

ADJECTIVE _____

PLURAL NOUN _____

ADJECTIVE _____

ADJECTIVE _____

NOUN _____

LAST NAME OF PERSON IN ROOM _____

LAST NAME OF PERSON IN ROOM _____

A PLACE _____

LAST NAME OF PERSON IN ROOM _____

PART OF THE BODY _____

TYPE OF LIQUID _____

ARTICLE OF CLOTHING (PLURAL) _____

RELATIVE _____

PIECE OF FURNITURE _____

VERB ENDING IN "ING" _____

ADJECTIVE _____

MAD LIBS®
CAMPFIRE STORIES

It is always fun to chop up some _____ and use them to build
_____PLURAL NOUN

a/an _____ campfire. Then you get all of the _____ to
_____ADJECTIVE_____PLURAL NOUN

sit around the fire and tell scary stories. You can tell about Ichabod Crane, the

_____ schoolteacher of Sleepy Hollow and his _____
____ADJECTIVE_____ADJECTIVE

adventures with the Headless _____. Or you can tell "The
_____NOUN

Fall of the House of _____," which was written by
_____LAST NAME OF PERSON IN ROOM

Edgar Allen _____. Or you can tell about vampires from
_____LAST NAME OF PERSON IN ROOM

(the) _____, like the terrible Count _____,
_____A PLACE_____LAST NAME OF PERSON IN ROOM

who bit people on the _____ and drank their _____.
_____PART OF THE BODY_____TYPE OF LIQUID

By this time, many of the young campers will start shaking in their

_____ and will begin yelling for their _____
ARTICLE OF CLOTHING (PLURAL)_____RELATIVE

and go hide under a _____. Believe me, when it comes to
_____PIECE OF FURNITURE

_____ a bunch of kids, there's nothing like a
_____VERB ENDING IN "ING"

really _____ ghost story.
_____ADJECTIVE

MAD LIBS® is fun to play with friends, but you can also play it by yourself! To begin with, DO NOT look at the story on the page below. Fill in the blanks on this page with the words called for. Then, using the words you have selected, fill in the blank spaces in the story.

Now you've created your own hilarious MAD LIBS® game!

A TOUR OF HOLLYWOOD

PLURAL NOUN _____

PLURAL NOUN _____

PERSON IN ROOM _____

NOUN _____

ADJECTIVE _____

NOUN _____

ADJECTIVE _____

ADJECTIVE _____

PLURAL NOUN _____

PART OF THE BODY _____

PLURAL NOUN _____

ADJECTIVE _____

NOUN _____

ADJECTIVE _____

PART OF THE BODY (PLURAL) _____

PLURAL NOUN _____

NOUN _____

PERSON IN ROOM _____

NUMBER _____

PART OF THE BODY (PLURAL) _____

MAD LIBS®
A TOUR OF HOLLYWOOD

Good morning, ladies and _____, boys and _____.
                                PLURAL NOUN   PLURAL NOUN

My name is _____. I am your personal _____ guide.
              PERSON IN ROOM   NOUN

For the next six hours, we will delight in exploring romantic, _____
                                                                  ADJECTIVE

Hollywood, the glamour _____ of the world. Let's start off
                              NOUN

with a bang and visit Grauman's _____ Theatre, Hollywood's
                                      ADJECTIVE

most _____ tourist attraction. You'll see etched in cement
        ADJECTIVE

the foot-_____ and _____-prints of the
            PLURAL NOUN   PART OF THE BODY

most famous movie _____ ever to adorn the _____
                        PLURAL NOUN   ADJECTIVE

screen. Then it's only a hop, skip, and a/an _____ to Beverly Hills,
                                                    NOUN

the playground of the rich and _____. You will feast your
                                      ADJECTIVE

_____ on the million dollar _____ of movie stars.
PART OF THE BODY (PLURAL)   PLURAL NOUN

You'll actually get to visit the home of today's hottest _____,
                                                              NOUN

_____, who will sign autographs for the low, low sum of
PERSON IN ROOM

_____ dollars each. And here's the big one! For lunch, we'll be going to
NUMBER

a studio commissary, where you can rub _____ with today's
                                            PART OF THE BODY (PLURAL)

leading actors and actresses. All aboard!

MAD LIBS® is fun to play with friends, but you can also play it by yourself! To begin with, DO NOT look at the story on the page below. Fill in the blanks on this page with the words called for. Then, using the words you have selected, fill in the blank spaces in the story.

Now you've created your own hilarious MAD LIBS® game!

FATHER GOOSE RHYMES

NOUN _____

ADJECTIVE _____

ANIMAL_____

SAME NOUN _____

ADJECTIVE _____

ADJECTIVE _____

NOUN _____

TYPE OF CONTAINER _____

NOUN _____

PART OF THE BODY _____

ADJECTIVE _____

ADJECTIVE _____

ADJECTIVE _____

ADJECTIVE _____

VERB (PAST TENSE) _____

PLURAL NOUN_____

MAD LIBS®
FATHER GOOSE RHYMES

Old Mother Hubbard went to the _____
NOUN

To get her _____ _____ a bone.
ADJECTIVE   ANIMAL

When she got there, the _____ was _____,
SAME NOUN   ADJECTIVE

And so her _____ dog had none.
ADJECTIVE

Jack and Jill went up the _____
NOUN

To fetch a/an _____ of water.
TYPE OF CONTAINER

Jack fell down and broke his _____,
NOUN

And Jill came tumbling after.

There was a little girl, and she had a little curl

Right in the middle of her _____.
PART OF THE BODY

And when she was _____, she was very, very _____,
ADJECTIVE   ADJECTIVE

And when she was bad, she was _____.
ADJECTIVE

There was a/an _____ woman
ADJECTIVE

Who _____ in a shoe.
VERB (PAST TENSE)

She had so many _____,
PLURAL NOUN

She didn't know what to do.

MAD LIBS® is fun to play with friends, but you can also play it by yourself! To begin with, DO NOT look at the story on the page below. Fill in the blanks on this page with the words called for. Then, using the words you have selected, fill in the blank spaces in the story.

Now you've created your own hilarious MAD LIBS® game!

MORE FATHER GOOSE RHYMES

NOUN _____

ANIMAL_____

NOUN THAT RHYMES WITH "MOON" _____

NOUN THAT RHYMES WITH "MOON" _____

NOUN _____

NOUN THAT RHYMES WITH "DAY"_____

ANIMAL_____

MUSICAL INSTRUMENT_____

A PLACE _____

TYPE OF VEGETABLE_____

ADJECTIVE _____

NOUN _____

ANIMAL_____

NOUN _____

SAME ANIMAL _____

VERB THAT RHYMES WITH "SNOW" _____

MAD LIBS®
MORE FATHER GOOSE RHYMES

Hey, diddle, diddle, the _____ and the fiddle,
NOUN

The _____ jumped over the _____.
ANIMAL   NOUN THAT RHYMES WITH "MOON"

The little dog laughed to see such sport,

And the dish ran away with the _____.
NOUN THAT RHYMES WITH "MOON"

Little Miss Muffet sat on a/an _____,
NOUN

Eating her curds and _____.
NOUN THAT RHYMES WITH "DAY"

Along came a/an _____ and sat down beside her
ANIMAL

And frightened Miss Muffet away.

Little Boy Blue, come blow your _____.
MUSICAL INSTRUMENT

The sheep's in (the) _____, the cow's in the _____.
A PLACE   TYPE OF VEGETABLE

Where is the _____ boy who looks after the sheep?
ADJECTIVE

He's under the _____, fast asleep.
NOUN

Mary had a little _____.
ANIMAL

Its _____ was white as snow.
NOUN

And everywhere that Mary went

The _____ was sure to _____.
SAME ANIMAL   VERB THAT RHYMES WITH "SNOW"

The stories in this book were originally published between 1958 and 2008 by Price Stern Sloan.
Copyright © Penguin Random House LLC.

MAD LIBS® is fun to play with friends, but you can also play it by yourself! To begin with, DO NOT look at the story on the page below. Fill in the blanks on this page with the words called for. Then, using the words you have selected, fill in the blank spaces in the story.

Now you've created your own hilarious MAD LIBS® game!

ALICE'S UPSIDE-DOWN WORLD

ADJECTIVE _____

NOUN _____

PLURAL NOUN_____

NUMBER _____

ADJECTIVE _____

VERB ENDING IN "S" _____

ADJECTIVE _____

NOUN _____

NOUN _____

NOUN _____

NOUN _____

VERB ENDING IN "S" _____

NOUN _____

ADJECTIVE _____

NOUN _____

PLURAL NOUN_____

ADJECTIVE _____

NOUN _____

MAD LIBS®
ALICE'S UPSIDE-DOWN WORLD

Lewis Carroll's classic, *Alice's Adventures in Wonderland*, as well as its

_____ sequel, *Through the Looking-*_____, have
　　　ADJECTIVE　　　　　　　　　　　　　　　　　　　NOUN

enchanted both young and old _____ for the last _____
　　　　　　　　　　　　　　　　　PLURAL NOUN　　　　　　　　　NUMBER

years. Alice's _____ adventures begin when she
　　　　　　　　　　　　ADJECTIVE

_____down a/an _____ hole and lands in
VERB ENDING IN "S"　　　　　　　ADJECTIVE

a strange and topsy-turvy _____. There, she discovers she can
　　　　　　　　　　　　　　NOUN

become a tall _____ or a small _____ simply
　　　　　　　NOUN　　　　　　　　　　　　NOUN

by nibbling on alternate sides of a magic _____. In her travels
　　　　　　　　　　　　　　　　　　　　NOUN

through Wonderland, Alice _____ with such remarkable
　　　　　　　　　　　VERB ENDING IN "S"

characters as the White _____, the _____
　　　　　　　　　　　　NOUN　　　　　　　　　　　ADJECTIVE

Hatter, the Cheshire _____, and even the Queen of _____.
　　　　　　　　　　NOUN　　　　　　　　　　　　　　　　PLURAL NOUN

Unfortunately, Alice's adventures come to a/an _____ end
　　　　　　　　　　　　　　　　　　　　　ADJECTIVE

when Alice awakens from her _____.
　　　　　　　　　　　　　NOUN

MAD LIBS® is fun to play with friends, but you can also play it by yourself! To begin with, DO NOT look at the story on the page below. Fill in the blanks on this page with the words called for. Then, using the words you have selected, fill in the blank spaces in the story.

Now you've created your own hilarious MAD LIBS® game!

HOW TO STUDY

ADJECTIVE _____

ADJECTIVE _____

NOUN _____

NOUN _____

PLURAL NOUN _____

ADVERB _____

VERB _____

ADJECTIVE _____

PLURAL NOUN _____

ADJECTIVE _____

ADJECTIVE _____

ADJECTIVE _____

PLURAL NOUN _____

MAD LIBS®
HOW TO STUDY

_____ teachers always give out _____ assignments.
     ADJECTIVE   ADJECTIVE

But as everyone knows, if you want to pass all your classes so you can go

to a/an _____ and become president of a big international
          NOUN

_____ and have millions of _____ in the
     NOUN   PLURAL NOUN

bank, you must do your homework and study _____. If you
                                         ADVERB

just sit around and _____, you won't get ahead in life. You
                       VERB

must learn to pay attention to every _____ thing your teacher
                               ADJECTIVE

says. Do not interrupt or whisper to other _____ during class.
                                 PLURAL NOUN

Be sure to have a nice, _____ notebook in which you can
                     ADJECTIVE

write down anything the teacher says that seems _____. Then
                                 ADJECTIVE

go home and memorize all of those _____ notes. When your
                            ADJECTIVE

teacher gives a surprise quiz, you will know all of the _____.
                                              PLURAL NOUN

MAD LIBS® is fun to play with friends, but you can also play it by yourself! To begin with, DO NOT look at the story on the page below. Fill in the blanks on this page with the words called for. Then, using the words you have selected, fill in the blank spaces in the story.

Now you've created your own hilarious MAD LIBS® game!

DRIVING TIPS

ADJECTIVE _____

NOUN _____

NOUN _____

ADJECTIVE _____

PART OF THE BODY _____

NOUN _____

NOUN _____

ADJECTIVE _____

PLURAL NOUN _____

ADVERB _____

NOUN _____

MAD LIBS®
DRIVING TIPS

Driving a car can be fun if you follow this _____ advice:
ADJECTIVE

1. When approaching a/an _____ on the right, always blow
NOUN

   your _____.
   NOUN

2. Before making a/an _____ turn, always stick your
ADJECTIVE

   _____ out the window.
   PART OF THE BODY

3. Every two thousand miles, have your _____ inspected and
NOUN

   your _____ checked.
   NOUN

4. When approaching a school, watch out for _____
ADJECTIVE

   _____.
   PLURAL NOUN

5. Above all, drive _____. The _____
ADVERB   NOUN

   you save may be your own.

MAD LIBS® is fun to play with friends, but you can also play it by yourself! To begin with, DO NOT look at the story on the page below. Fill in the blanks on this page with the words called for. Then, using the words you have selected, fill in the blank spaces in the story.

Now you've created your own hilarious MAD LIBS® game!

THE STOCK MARKET (CAPITALISM MADE EASY)

PLURAL NOUN _____

ADJECTIVE _____

SAME PLURAL NOUN _____

ANIMAL_____

NOUN _____

ADJECTIVE _____

ADJECTIVE _____

PLURAL NOUN _____

NOUN _____

ADJECTIVE _____

NOUN _____

NOUN _____

ADJECTIVE _____

NOUN _____

PLURAL NOUN _____

ADJECTIVE _____

NOUN _____

MAD LIBS®

THE STOCK MARKET (CAPITALISM MADE EASY)

This is how I made one million _____ in the stock market. It's

PLURAL NOUN

simple. At the present time, any _____ investor with a little

ADJECTIVE

capital should be able to double his _____ in a few months.

SAME PLURAL NOUN

All the experts agree that we are nearing the end of the _____

ANIMAL

market. Just recently, for instance, the American _____ and

NOUN

Foundry Company has shown a/an _____ trend. Conditions

ADJECTIVE

indicate a/an _____ market for their principal product,

ADJECTIVE

automatic _____. International Telephone and _____

PLURAL NOUN — NOUN

Company also looks _____. At the end of the last fiscal

ADJECTIVE

_____, they were earning ten dollars a/an _____.

NOUN — NOUN

Another _____ tip is Consolidated _____.

ADJECTIVE — NOUN

This outfit manufactures and sells electronic _____ of a very

PLURAL NOUN

_____ quality. But whatever you do, act now. Remember,

ADJECTIVE

prosperity is just around the _____.

NOUN

MAD LIBS® is fun to play with friends, but you can also play it by yourself! To begin with, DO NOT look at the story on the page below. Fill in the blanks on this page with the words called for. Then, using the words you have selected, fill in the blank spaces in the story.

Now you've created your own hilarious MAD LIBS® game!

HOW TO DATE THE COOLEST GUY/GIRL IN SCHOOL

PLURAL NOUN _____

ADVERB _____

VERB _____

ARTICLE OF CLOTHING _____

PART OF THE BODY _____

ADJECTIVE _____

NOUN _____

PLURAL NOUN _____

PART OF THE BODY _____

PLURAL NOUN _____

PART OF THE BODY _____

NOUN _____

NOUN _____

VERB ENDING IN "ING" _____

ADJECTIVE _____

ADJECTIVE _____

VERB _____

MAD LIBS®

HOW TO DATE THE COOLEST GUY/GIRL IN SCHOOL

It's simple: Turn the _____ and make him/her want _____
                                    PLURAL NOUN   ADVERB

to date you. Make sure you're always dressed to _____. Each
                                                                                         VERB

and every day, wear a/an _____ that you know shows off your
                                          ARTICLE OF CLOTHING

_____ to _____ advantage and makes
        PART OF THE BODY   ADJECTIVE

your _____ look like a million _____. Even
                NOUN   PLURAL NOUN

if the two of you make meaningful _____ contact, don't admit it.
                                                               PART OF THE BODY

No hugs or _____. Just shake his/her _____
                        PLURAL NOUN   PART OF THE BODY

firmly. And remember, when he/she asks you out, even though a chill may run

down your _____ and you won't be able to stop your _____
                        NOUN   NOUN

from _____, just play it _____. Take a long
            VERB ENDING IN "ING"   ADJECTIVE

pause before answering in a very _____ voice, "I'll have to
                                                          ADJECTIVE

_____ it over."
        VERB

The stories in this book were originally published between 1958 and 2008 by Price Stern Sloan.

MAD LIBS® is fun to play with friends, but you can also play it by yourself! To begin with, DO NOT look at the story on the page below. Fill in the blanks on this page with the words called for. Then, using the words you have selected, fill in the blank spaces in the story.

Now you've created your own hilarious MAD LIBS® game!

HAVE I GOT
A GIRAFFE FOR YOU!

PLURAL NOUN _____

PLURAL NOUN _____

PART OF THE BODY _____

NUMBER _____

PLURAL NOUN _____

PART OF THE BODY _____

TYPE OF LIQUID _____

PART OF THE BODY (PLURAL) _____

PART OF THE BODY _____

ADJECTIVE _____

PLURAL NOUN _____

ADJECTIVE _____

ADJECTIVE _____

VERB ENDING IN "ING" _____

NOUN _____

PLURAL NOUN _____

NOUN _____

MAD LIBS®
HAVE I GOT A GIRAFFE FOR YOU!

Giraffes have aroused the curiosity of _____ since earliest

PLURAL NOUN

times. The giraffe is the tallest of all living _____, but scientists

PLURAL NOUN

are unable to explain how it got its long _____. The giraffe's

PART OF THE BODY

tremendous height, which can reach up to _____ _____,

NUMBER   PLURAL NOUN

comes mostly from its legs and _____. If a giraffe wants to

PART OF THE BODY

take a drink of _____ from the ground, it has to spread its

TYPE OF LIQUID

_____ far apart in order to reach down and lap up the water

PART OF THE BODY (PLURAL)

with its huge _____. The giraffe has _____

PART OF THE BODY   ADJECTIVE

ears that are sensitive to the faintest _____, and it has

PLURAL NOUN

_____ senses of smell and sight. When attacked, a giraffe can put

ADJECTIVE

up a/an _____ fight by _____ out with

ADJECTIVE   VERB ENDING IN "ING"

its hind legs and using its head like a sledge-_____. Finally, a

NOUN

giraffe can gallop at more than thirty _____ per hour when

PLURAL NOUN

pursued, and can outrun the fastest _____.

NOUN

MAD LIBS® is fun to play with friends, but you can also play it by yourself! To begin with, DO NOT look at the story on the page below. Fill in the blanks on this page with the words called for. Then, using the words you have selected, fill in the blank spaces in the story.

Now you've created your own hilarious MAD LIBS® game!

HISTORY OF A FAMOUS INVENTION

NOUN _____

ADJECTIVE _____

CELEBRITY (MALE) _____

CELEBRITY (MALE) _____

PLURAL NOUN_____

EXCLAMATION _____

NOUN _____

ADJECTIVE _____

PLURAL NOUN_____

NOUN _____

TYPE OF FOOD _____

TYPE OF LIQUID_____

NOUN _____

ADJECTIVE _____

NUMBER _____

ADVERB _____

MAD LIBS®

HISTORY OF A FAMOUS INVENTION

The first electric _____ was invented in 1904 by a/an
                              NOUN

_____ young man named _____. He
     ADJECTIVE   CELEBRITY (MALE)

and his brother, _____, ran a small repair shop, and in their
                      CELEBRITY (MALE)

spare time they studied _____. When they started to work
                              PLURAL NOUN

on their invention, everyone said, "_____! You'll never get it
                                          EXCLAMATION

off the _____." But they built a/an _____
              NOUN   ADJECTIVE

model out of old _____ and a used _____.
                        PLURAL NOUN   NOUN

The model worked fine, and in ten minutes it toasted twenty-four slices of

_____. It also used up two gallons of _____
     TYPE OF FOOD   TYPE OF LIQUID

per hour, and the top converted into a/an _____. The brothers
                                                  NOUN

sold the patent to a/an _____ millionaire for _____
                              ADJECTIVE   NUMBER

dollars and lived _____ ever after.
                        ADVERB

MAD LIBS® is fun to play with friends, but you can also play it by yourself! To begin with, DO NOT look at the story on the page below. Fill in the blanks on this page with the words called for. Then, using the words you have selected, fill in the blank spaces in the story.

Now you've created your own hilarious MAD LIBS® game!

HOW CAN I TELL
IF SHE LIKES ME?

ADJECTIVE _____

PART OF THE BODY _____

ADVERB _____

NOUN _____

NUMBER _____

NOUN _____

NOUN _____

NUMBER _____

NOUN _____

NOUN _____

PLURAL NOUN_____

NOUN _____

ADJECTIVE _____

NOUN _____

PART OF THE BODY _____

PLURAL NOUN_____

MAD LIBS®
HOW CAN I TELL IF SHE LIKES ME?

Keep your eyes open for these _____ signs:
ADJECTIVE

1. On your first date she fusses with her _____ a lot and
PART OF THE BODY

   giggles _____ at everything you say.
   ADVERB

2. When you pick her up at her _____, she keeps you waiting
NOUN

   for _____ minutes. (You later learn that she changed her
   NUMBER

   _____ ten times.)
   NOUN

3. When you're alone at a restaurant, she gets up from the _____
NOUN

   every _____ minutes to visit the ladies' _____. (You
   NUMBER   NOUN

   can safely bet she's calling her best _____.)
   NOUN

4. She starts to flirt with other _____ when you don't give
PLURAL NOUN

   her your full _____.
   NOUN

5. A/An _____ friend of hers happens to run into you "accidentally"
   ADJECTIVE

   and tells you her friend thinks you're a cool _____.
   NOUN

6. She draws a/an _____ and puts her initials and your
   PART OF THE BODY

   _____ in it.
   PLURAL NOUN

MAD LIBS® is fun to play with friends, but you can also play it by yourself! To begin with, DO NOT look at the story on the page below. Fill in the blanks on this page with the words called for. Then, using the words you have selected, fill in the blank spaces in the story.

Now you've created your own hilarious MAD LIBS® game!

HOW CAN I TELL IF HE LIKES ME?

PLURAL NOUN _____

ADVERB _____

TYPE OF FRUIT _____

PART OF THE BODY _____

PLURAL NOUN _____

NOUN _____

NOUN _____

COLOR _____

NOUN _____

VERB ENDING IN "ING" _____

PART OF THE BODY _____

PLURAL NOUN _____

VERB _____

VERB _____

NOUN _____

PLURAL NOUN _____

NOUN _____

PLURAL NOUN _____

MAD LIBS®
HOW CAN I TELL IF HE LIKES ME?

If he exhibits three or more of the following _____, you may

_____ assume you are the _____ of his eye.
    ADVERB   TYPE OF FRUIT

(above blank: PLURAL NOUN)

1. When you look him straight in the _____, does he avert his
                                         PART OF THE BODY

   _____ and give you an uncomfortable _____?
   PLURAL NOUN   NOUN

2. If you compliment him, does his _____ turn bright
                                       NOUN

   _____?
   COLOR

3. After you first met, did he call a mutual _____ to see if you
                                         NOUN

   were _____ steady?
          VERB ENDING IN "ING"

4. When you were alone for the first time, did he try to put his

   _____ around you? Did you find his _____
   PART OF THE BODY   PLURAL NOUN

   wet and clammy, and did he sweat and _____ excessively?
                                      VERB

5. After a passionate date, does he _____ you on the phone
                                     VERB

   or write you a/an _____, or better yet, send you a bouquet
                   NOUN

   of _____?
        PLURAL NOUN

If he did three or more of the above, you can bet your last _____
                                                         NOUN

he has the _____ for you.
         PLURAL NOUN

MAD LIBS® is fun to play with friends, but you can also play it by yourself! To begin with, DO NOT look at the story on the page below. Fill in the blanks on this page with the words called for. Then, using the words you have selected, fill in the blank spaces in the story.

Now you've created your own hilarious MAD LIBS® game!

PORTRAIT OF GREAT-GRANDMA

NOUN _____

NOUN _____

ADJECTIVE _____

NOUN _____

NOUN _____

NOUN _____

ADJECTIVE _____

PLURAL NOUN_____

PART OF THE BODY (PLURAL) _____

ADJECTIVE _____

PLURAL NOUN_____

PLURAL NOUN_____

ADJECTIVE _____

NOUN _____

ADJECTIVE _____

MAD LIBS®
PORTRAIT OF GREAT-GRANDMA

A striking painting of Great-Grandma as a young _____ has been
                                                        NOUN

hanging in our living _____ for as long as I can remember. A
                            NOUN

local art dealer believes it was painted by James McNeill Whistler, whose most

_____ work is the painting of his _____
        ADJECTIVE   NOUN

sitting in a rocking _____. It could be true. After all,
                              NOUN

Great-Grandma was the reigning _____ of her day.
                                              NOUN

With her _____ complexion, high cheek-_____,
              ADJECTIVE   PLURAL NOUN

and vivid green _____, there wasn't a portrait artist alive
                    PART OF THE BODY (PLURAL)

who didn't want to paint her. And she had no end of _____
                                                                ADJECTIVE

suitors. Over the years she was courted by crowned _____ of
                                                            PLURAL NOUN

Europe as well as the leading _____ of American society.
                                      PLURAL NOUN

I've often wondered why she married Great-Grandpa, because to tell the truth,

he was kind of _____-looking. When I asked Dad about it, he said
                      ADJECTIVE

that Great-Grandpa was the only _____ who could make her
                                              NOUN

laugh. Isn't love _____?!
                        ADJECTIVE

MAD LIBS® is fun to play with friends, but you can also play it by yourself! To begin with, DO NOT look at the story on the page below. Fill in the blanks on this page with the words called for. Then, using the words you have selected, fill in the blank spaces in the story.

Now you've created your own hilarious MAD LIBS® game!

MOONWALKING

VERB ENDING IN "ING" _____

NUMBER _____

PERSON IN ROOM _____

NOUN _____

PERSON IN ROOM _____

OCCUPATION _____

ADJECTIVE _____

COLOR _____

PLURAL NOUN _____

TYPE OF DAIRY FOOD _____

MAD LIBS®
MOONWALKING

The greatest true-life space story is the one about our astronauts

_____ on the moon for the first time. There were
VERB ENDING IN "ING"

_____ astronauts. We all remember their names: _____,
NUMBER   PERSON IN ROOM

who was the expert in _____, and _____,
NOUN   PERSON IN ROOM

who was the ship's _____ and conducted a series of really
OCCUPATION

_____ experiments with _____ mice and
ADJECTIVE   COLOR

_____. It was a great day for America when they landed and
PLURAL NOUN

said, "Whatta ya know? It really is made out of _____."
TYPE OF DAIRY FOOD

MAD LIBS® is fun to play with friends, but you can also play it by yourself! To begin with, DO NOT look at the story on the page below. Fill in the blanks on this page with the words called for. Then, using the words you have selected, fill in the blank spaces in the story.

Now you've created your own hilarious MAD LIBS® game!

FIGURE SKATING

PLURAL NOUN _____

ADVERB _____

PERSON IN ROOM (FEMALE) _____

NOUN _____

NOUN _____

ADJECTIVE _____

ADJECTIVE _____

ADJECTIVE _____

NOUN _____

VERB _____

ADJECTIVE _____

NOUN _____

NOUN _____

NOUN _____

ADJECTIVE _____

NOUN _____

PLURAL NOUN _____

NOUN _____

MAD LIBS®
FIGURE SKATING

As a crowd of more than nineteen thousand _____ filed into
PLURAL NOUN

the _____ designed auditorium, _____,
ADVERB   PERSON IN ROOM (FEMALE)

our _____-skating champion, went through her warm-up
NOUN

_____. For the first time in her _____ life,
NOUN   ADJECTIVE

the champion felt frightened and _____. As the music began,
ADJECTIVE

the champion took a/an _____ breath, smoothed the ruffles
ADJECTIVE

of her _____, and started to _____. Just
NOUN   VERB

as she feared, when it came time for her most _____ jump, a
ADJECTIVE

triple _____, she lost her balance and landed with a thump
NOUN

on her _____. She stood up bravely, brushed the ice off of her
NOUN

_____, and finished her _____ routine. The
NOUN   ADJECTIVE

crowd gave her a five-minute standing _____. Even though
NOUN

she realized she had lost the competition, she knew she had won the hearts and

_____ of every _____ in the auditorium.
PLURAL NOUN   NOUN

MAD LIBS® is fun to play with friends, but you can also play it by yourself! To begin with, DO NOT look at the story on the page below. Fill in the blanks on this page with the words called for. Then, using the words you have selected, fill in the blank spaces in the story.

Now you've created your own hilarious MAD LIBS® game!

OUR YEARBOOK

ADJECTIVE _____

EXCLAMATION _____

VERB (PAST TENSE) _____

VERB (PAST TENSE) _____

ADVERB _____

TYPE OF SPORT _____

SILLY WORD (PLURAL) _____

LANGUAGE_____

PLURAL NOUN_____

NUMBER _____

PERSON IN ROOM (MALE) _____

PERSON IN ROOM (FEMALE) _____

OCCUPATION_____

ADJECTIVE _____

OCCUPATION (PLURAL)_____

VERB ENDING IN "ING"_____

PLURAL NOUN_____

VERB _____

PLURAL NOUN_____

PART OF THE BODY _____

MAD LIBS®
OUR YEARBOOK

On the last day of school, our _____ yearbooks came out.
                                    ADJECTIVE

Everyone yelled "_____!" and _____ to
                        EXCLAMATION   VERB (PAST TENSE)

grab one. When we _____ it, we couldn't believe
                        VERB (PAST TENSE)

how _____ it came out! It was filled with pictures of our
            ADVERB

_____ team, the _____; the _____
    TYPE OF SPORT   SILLY WORD (PLURAL)   LANGUAGE

club; and our school marching band, the _____. There were
                                            PLURAL NOUN

_____ pages devoted to Homecoming, where _____
    NUMBER   PERSON IN ROOM (MALE)

and _____ were named king and _____.
        PERSON IN ROOM (FEMALE)   OCCUPATION

There were even snapshots of our _____ _____.
                                    ADJECTIVE   OCCUPATION (PLURAL)

After we finished _____ through all of the cool _____,
                    VERB ENDING IN "ING"   PLURAL NOUN

everyone grabbed pens so we could _____ one another's books. I
                                        VERB

signed so many _____, I thought my _____
                    PLURAL NOUN   PART OF THE BODY

would fall off!

MAD LIBS® is fun to play with friends, but you can also play it by yourself! To begin with, DO NOT look at the story on the page below. Fill in the blanks on this page with the words called for. Then, using the words you have selected, fill in the blank spaces in the story.

Now you've created your own hilarious MAD LIBS® game!

SUPER-CHICKENS

ADJECTIVE _____

VERB _____

PLURAL NOUN _____

PART OF THE BODY _____

VERB _____

PLURAL NOUN _____

ADJECTIVE _____

A PLACE _____

PLURAL NOUN _____

OCCUPATION _____

SILLY WORD _____

A PLACE _____

PLURAL NOUN _____

ADJECTIVE _____

SILLY WORD _____

VERB _____

MAD LIBS®
SUPER-CHICKENS

One of my favorite shows on TV is *Super-Chickens*. It's about three chickens that

each have _____ superpowers. One of them can _____,
         ADJECTIVE   VERB

another one can shoot _____ from her _____,
                         PLURAL NOUN   PART OF THE BODY

and the third one can _____ with _____.
                         VERB   PLURAL NOUN

The Super-Chickens use their powers to protect the _____
                                                ADJECTIVE

people of (the) _____ and defeat the powers of _____.
                A PLACE   PLURAL NOUN

My favorite episode is when their father is kidnapped by the evil _____,
                                                    OCCUPATION

Mr. _____, and they have to fly to (the) _____
        SILLY WORD   A PLACE

to rescue him. In another episode, the Super-Chickens have to fight a villain

who is made out of _____. The show is so cool that I even bought
                  PLURAL NOUN

a/an _____ *Super-Chickens* T-shirt and a watch that says
               ADJECTIVE

"_____ to the rescue—Super-Chickens!" when you _____
      SILLY WORD   VERB

a button.

MAD LIBS® is fun to play with friends, but you can also play it by yourself! To begin with, DO NOT look at the story on the page below. Fill in the blanks on this page with the words called for. Then, using the words you have selected, fill in the blank spaces in the story.

Now you've created your own hilarious MAD LIBS® game!

POLITICAL SPEECH

ADJECTIVE _____

ADJECTIVE _____

PLURAL NOUN _____

PLURAL NOUN _____

ADJECTIVE _____

NOUN _____

NOUN _____

PLURAL NOUN _____

ADJECTIVE _____

PERSON IN ROOM (MALE) _____

ADJECTIVE _____

NOUN _____

ADJECTIVE _____

NOUN _____

PLURAL NOUN _____

PLURAL NOUN _____

ADJECTIVE _____

ADJECTIVE _____

ADJECTIVE _____

MAD LIBS®
POLITICAL SPEECH

Ladies and gentlemen, on this _____ occasion, it is a privilege

ADJECTIVE

to address such a/an _____-looking group of _____.

ADJECTIVE   PLURAL NOUN

I can tell from your smiling _____ that you will support my

PLURAL NOUN

_____ program in the coming election. I promise that, if

ADJECTIVE

elected, there will be a/an _____ in every _____,

NOUN   NOUN

and two _____ in every garage. I want to warn you against my

PLURAL NOUN

_____ opponent, Mr. _____. The man is

ADJECTIVE   PERSON IN ROOM (MALE)

nothing but a/an _____ _____. He has

ADJECTIVE   NOUN

a/an _____ character and is working _____

ADJECTIVE   NOUN

in glove with the criminal element. If elected, I promise to eliminate vice. I will

keep _____ off the city's streets. I will keep crooks from dipping

PLURAL NOUN

their _____ in the public till. I promise you _____

PLURAL NOUN   ADJECTIVE

government, _____ taxes, and _____ schools.

ADJECTIVE   ADJECTIVE

MAD LIBS® is fun to play with friends, but you can also play it by yourself! To begin with, DO NOT look at the story on the page below. Fill in the blanks on this page with the words called for. Then, using the words you have selected, fill in the blank spaces in the story.

Now you've created your own hilarious MAD LIBS® game!

CONFESSIONS OF A PIZZA EATER

NATIONALITY _____

CELEBRITY_____

TYPE OF MATERIAL _____

ADJECTIVE _____

TYPE OF LIQUID_____

PLURAL NOUN_____

TYPE OF FOOD _____

NOUN _____

VERB _____

ADJECTIVE _____

ADJECTIVE _____

TYPE OF FANCY FOOD _____

NUMBER _____

The pizza was invented by a famous _____ chef named
NATIONALITY

_____. To make a pizza, you take a lump of _____
CELEBRITY   TYPE OF MATERIAL

and make a thin, round, _____ pancake. Then you cover it with
ADJECTIVE

tomato _____, Parmesan _____, and pieces
TYPE OF LIQUID   PLURAL NOUN

of _____. Next you bake it in a very hot _____.
TYPE OF FOOD   NOUN

Then you _____ it and slice it into wedges. Some people like
VERB

_____ pizzas best. My favorite is the _____
ADJECTIVE   ADJECTIVE

pizza. My mother says that pizza is junk food, but I think it is better than

_____. If I could, I would eat pizza _____
TYPE OF FANCY FOOD   NUMBER

times a day.

MAD LIBS® is fun to play with friends, but you can also play it by yourself! To begin with, DO NOT look at the story on the page below. Fill in the blanks on this page with the words called for. Then, using the words you have selected, fill in the blank spaces in the story.

Now you've created your own hilarious MAD LIBS® game!

HOW TO SERVE A TENNIS BALL . . . OR EVEN LUNCH

ADJECTIVE _____

NOUN _____

NOUN _____

ADVERB _____

PART OF THE BODY _____

PART OF THE BODY (PLURAL) _____

NOUN _____

NOUN _____

ADJECTIVE _____

ADJECTIVE _____

PART OF THE BODY _____

NOUN _____

NOUN _____

ADJECTIVE _____

NOUN _____

MAD LIBS®

HOW TO SERVE A TENNIS BALL . . . OR EVEN LUNCH

Here are some _____ suggestions to help improve your tennis
                    ADJECTIVE

_____.
        NOUN

1. As you bounce your _____, imagine where you want it to land.
                           NOUN

   Keep this image _____ in your _____.
                        ADVERB   PART OF THE BODY

2. By bending your _____, you are able to push off the
                    PART OF THE BODY (PLURAL)

   _____ and put more of your _____ into
          NOUN   NOUN

   your _____ serve.
            ADJECTIVE

3. Remember, if you have relaxed and _____ muscles, you
                                          ADJECTIVE

   can let your _____ snap like a/an _____
                 PART OF THE BODY   NOUN

   and serve a/an _____.
                        NOUN

If you follow this _____ advice, in no time you can be a
                        ADJECTIVE

Wimbledon _____.
                NOUN

MAD LIBS® is fun to play with friends, but you can also play it by yourself! To begin with, DO NOT look at the story on the page below. Fill in the blanks on this page with the words called for. Then, using the words you have selected, fill in the blank spaces in the story.

Now you've created your own hilarious MAD LIBS® game!

SCENE FROM A HORROR PICTURE

PERSON IN ROOM (MALE) _____

ADJECTIVE _____

HOLIDAY _____

NOUN _____

PLURAL NOUN _____

NOUN _____

PART OF THE BODY _____

SCHOOL SUBJECT _____

SCHOOL _____

NOUN _____

ADJECTIVE _____

NOUN _____

MAD LIBS®
SCENE FROM A HORROR PICTURE

To be read aloud by a male and a female.

GIRL: Oh, _____, why did we have to come to this
PERSON IN ROOM (MALE)

_____ old castle?
ADJECTIVE

BOY: All the hotels were closed because of _____.
HOLIDAY

GIRL: Just look at that sign. It says "The Howard Dracula Holiday _____."
NOUN

BOY: Here comes the bellboy for our _____.
PLURAL NOUN

GIRL: My, he is bent over and has a big _____ riding on his
NOUN

_____.
PART OF THE BODY

BOY: I think he is my old _____ teacher from _____.
SCHOOL SUBJECT   SCHOOL

GIRL: Watch out! He's throwing a/an _____ over your head.
NOUN

BOY: No, no. He's just being _____.
ADJECTIVE

GIRL: Now he's dragging you toward a bottomless _____!
NOUN

BOY: I was right—it *is* my old teacher. Help!

MAD LIBS® is fun to play with friends, but you can also play it by yourself! To begin with, DO NOT look at the story on the page below. Fill in the blanks on this page with the words called for. Then, using the words you have selected, fill in the blank spaces in the story.

Now you've created your own hilarious MAD LIBS® game!

TV REVIEW

ADJECTIVE _____

ADJECTIVE _____

VERB ENDING IN "S" _____

THREE LETTERS OF THE ALPHABET _____

NUMBER _____

NOUN _____

ADJECTIVE _____

ADJECTIVE _____

NOUN _____

NOUN _____

ADJECTIVE _____

ADJECTIVE _____

PLURAL NOUN_____

VERB _____

PLURAL NOUN_____

MAD LIBS®
TV REVIEW

As all of us know, the majority of _____ programs on television
<small>ADJECTIVE</small>

today are _____ comedies. Tonight, *The Prehistoric*
<small>ADJECTIVE</small>

Dinosaur Who _____ *People* made its debut on the
<small>VERB ENDING IN "S"</small>

_____ network at _____ o'clock. Part
<small>THREE LETTERS OF THE ALPHABET</small>   <small>NUMBER</small>

comedy and part science _____, tonight's episode follows the
<small>NOUN</small>

_____ adventures of four _____ students whose
<small>ADJECTIVE</small>   <small>ADJECTIVE</small>

boat sinks in the Sea of _____, leaving them stranded on a desert
<small>NOUN</small>

_____. Although the writing is _____, the directing is
<small>NOUN</small>   <small>ADJECTIVE</small>

_____, and the actors are a bunch of _____, there are
<small>ADJECTIVE</small>   <small>PLURAL NOUN</small>

moments in the show when you will _____ out loud. Our
<small>VERB</small>

rating: three _____.
<small>PLURAL NOUN</small>

MAD LIBS® is fun to play with friends, but you can also play it by yourself! To begin with, DO NOT look at the story on the page below. Fill in the blanks on this page with the words called for. Then, using the words you have selected, fill in the blank spaces in the story.

Now you've created your own hilarious MAD LIBS® game!

QUICK QUIZ

ADJECTIVE _____

NUMBER _____

GEOGRAPHICAL LOCATION _____

EXCLAMATION _____

NUMBER _____

ADJECTIVE _____

ADJECTIVE _____

PLURAL NOUN_____

ADVERB _____

ADJECTIVE _____

PERSON IN ROOM _____

NOUN _____

PLURAL NOUN_____

ADJECTIVE _____

NOUN _____

PERSON IN ROOM _____

MAD LIBS®
QUICK QUIZ

Who am I? I am a/an _____ American. I was born _____
                         ADJECTIVE   NUMBER

years ago in _____. When my father first saw me, he said,
              GEOGRAPHICAL LOCATION

"_____!" I am _____ feet tall and have
    EXCLAMATION   NUMBER

_____ brown eyes and a/an _____ complexion. My
    ADJECTIVE   ADJECTIVE

hobby is collecting _____. I always speak _____,
                      PLURAL NOUN   ADVERB

and I have made several _____ motion pictures. I am married
                              ADJECTIVE

to _____, the well-known Hollywood _____.
    PERSON IN ROOM   NOUN

I have given away thousands of _____ to charity. My most
                                  PLURAL NOUN

prominent physical characteristics are my _____ nose and my
                                             ADJECTIVE

large _____. Who am I?
        NOUN

ANSWER: I am _____.
              PERSON IN ROOM

MAD LIBS® is fun to play with friends, but you can also play it by yourself! To begin with, DO NOT look at the story on the page below. Fill in the blanks on this page with the words called for. Then, using the words you have selected, fill in the blank spaces in the story.

Now you've created your own hilarious MAD LIBS® game!

REVIEW OF
A MONSTER MOVIE

NOUN _____

ADJECTIVE _____

CELEBRITY (MALE) _____

ADJECTIVE _____

ADJECTIVE _____

PLURAL NOUN _____

PLURAL NOUN _____

COLOR _____

NUMBER _____

CELEBRITY _____

CELEBRITY (FEMALE) _____

CITY _____

CELEBRITY _____

ADVERB _____

MAD LIBS®

REVIEW OF A MONSTER MOVIE

A new movie has just opened called *The Teenage* _____ *Meets*
                                                    NOUN

the _____ *Vampire from Outer Space.* At the opening, we see
         ADJECTIVE

the teenage hero, played by _____, who is a/an _____
                              CELEBRITY (MALE)   ADJECTIVE

scientist. He is trying to build a/an _____ monster out of old
                                        ADJECTIVE

_____ and used _____. The monster has
   PLURAL NOUN   PLURAL NOUN

_____ skin and _____ arms and is played
      COLOR   NUMBER

by _____. Suddenly, the monster comes to life and kidnaps
      CELEBRITY

the beautiful heroine, played by _____. Then it begins to
                                    CELEBRITY (FEMALE)

destroy _____. In the end, the monster is destroyed by the
           CITY

vampire, who is played by _____. The hero and the heroine live
                            CELEBRITY

_____ ever after.
      ADVERB

MAD LIBS® is fun to play with friends, but you can also play it by yourself! To begin with, DO NOT look at the story on the page below. Fill in the blanks on this page with the words called for. Then, using the words you have selected, fill in the blank spaces in the story.

Now you've created your own hilarious MAD LIBS® game!

COMPUTER LAB

ADJECTIVE _____

NOUN _____

CELEBRITY (MALE) _____

NOUN _____

SOMETHING ALIVE _____

A PLACE _____

SAME CELEBRITY (MALE) _____

ADJECTIVE _____

PERSON IN ROOM (FEMALE) _____

ADJECTIVE _____

VERB ENDING IN "ING" _____

NOUN _____

VERB (PAST TENSE) _____

CITY _____

PLURAL NOUN _____

NUMBER _____

SAME PLACE _____

TYPE OF FOOD (PLURAL) _____

NOUN _____

PLURAL NOUN

MAD LIBS®
COMPUTER LAB

I love our computer lab at school. It's so _____! Every morning
ADJECTIVE

after _____ class, our teacher _____ takes
NOUN   CELEBRITY (MALE)

us to the lab so we can work on cool class projects like finding out who is

the oldest _____ or what a/an _____ eats for
NOUN   SOMETHING ALIVE

breakfast. Last week, our assignment was to research how many people live in

(the) _____. Since _____ always lets us
A PLACE   SAME CELEBRITY (MALE)

pick our _____ partners, I chose _____, because
ADJECTIVE   PERSON IN ROOM (FEMALE)

she's so _____. We had the best time _____ on
ADJECTIVE   VERB ENDING IN "ING"

the Internet. We found the coolest _____ that had all the
NOUN

information we needed. We _____ awesome facts about cities
VERB (PAST TENSE)

like _____ and all the _____ that live in them.
CITY   PLURAL NOUN

Can you believe that _____ people live in (the) _____?
NUMBER   SAME PLACE

And that they love to eat _____ for breakfast, lunch, and
TYPE OF FOOD (PLURAL)

_____? That's a lot of _____!
NOUN   PLURAL NOUN

MAD LIBS® is fun to play with friends, but you can also play it by yourself! To begin with, DO NOT look at the story on the page below. Fill in the blanks on this page with the words called for. Then, using the words you have selected, fill in the blank spaces in the story.

Now you've created your own hilarious MAD LIBS® game!

PAUL REVERE

STATE _____

ADJECTIVE _____

NOUN _____

NATIONALITY _____

NOUN _____

TYPE OF LIQUID_____

A PLACE_____

NOUN _____

NOUN _____

NOUN _____

ADVERB _____

PLURAL NOUN_____

SAME PLURAL NOUN _____

CELEBRITY (MALE) _____

MAD LIBS®
PAUL REVERE

Paul Revere was born in Boston, _____, in 1735. His father
                                         STATE

taught him to work with metals, and he soon became a/an _____
                                                                ADJECTIVE

_____. He was a soldier in the French and _____
        NOUN   NATIONALITY

War, and he was at the famous Boston _____ Party,
                                              NOUN

where American colonists dressed as Native Americans dumped tons of

_____ into the harbor. On April 18, 1775, Paul Revere waited
    TYPE OF LIQUID

in (the) _____ for a signal light from a church tower. The signal
          A PLACE

was to be one if by _____, two if by _____. When he
                        NOUN   NOUN

got the message, he mounted his faithful _____ and rode off
                                                  NOUN

_____. On the way, he kept yelling, "The _____ are
    ADVERB   PLURAL NOUN

coming! The _____ are coming!" This was the beginning of the
              SAME PLURAL NOUN

American War of Independence from King _____.
                                            CELEBRITY (MALE)

MAD LIBS® is fun to play with friends, but you can also play it by yourself! To begin with, DO NOT look at the story on the page below. Fill in the blanks on this page with the words called for. Then, using the words you have selected, fill in the blank spaces in the story.

Now you've created your own hilarious MAD LIBS® game!

HOW TO THROW A PIRATE PARTY

ADJECTIVE _____

NOUN _____

NOUN _____

PLURAL NOUN_____

ADJECTIVE _____

PLURAL NOUN_____

PLURAL NOUN_____

ADJECTIVE _____

NOUN _____

ADJECTIVE _____

PART OF THE BODY (PLURAL) _____

PART OF THE BODY (PLURAL) _____

NOUN _____

PERSON IN ROOM _____

NOUN _____

ADJECTIVE _____

MAD LIBS®
HOW TO THROW A PIRATE PARTY

If you are looking for a/an _____ way to celebrate your next
                                    ADJECTIVE

birthday, how about a pirate-themed costume party? Start by sending invitations

in the form of a buried _____ map with an X marking the
                                    NOUN

location of your _____. Make a sign for the front door that reads
                          NOUN

"Ahoy, _____," and fill the house with lots of _____
              PLURAL NOUN   ADJECTIVE

booty—Mom's silk _____, satin _____, and
                          PLURAL NOUN   PLURAL NOUN

_____ costume jewelry for starters. As your guests come aboard,
      ADJECTIVE

tie bandannas around their _____, place _____ patches
                                    NOUN   ADJECTIVE

over their _____, and give them fake tattoos for their arms
              PART OF THE BODY (PLURAL)

and _____. And remember, when the cake is presented,
        PART OF THE BODY (PLURAL)

sing a rousing version of "Happy birthday, dear _____-face
                                                          NOUN

_____!" Then, and only then, may you cut the chocolate
      PERSON IN ROOM

_____ with your _____ sword.
      NOUN   ADJECTIVE

MAD LIBS® is fun to play with friends, but you can also play it by yourself! To begin with, DO NOT look at the story on the page below. Fill in the blanks on this page with the words called for. Then, using the words you have selected, fill in the blank spaces in the story.

Now you've created your own hilarious MAD LIBS® game!

LETTER TO A FRIEND BACK HOME

PERSON IN ROOM _____

ADJECTIVE _____

A PLACE _____

ADJECTIVE _____

NUMBER _____

TYPE OF FOOD _____

PLURAL NOUN _____

ADJECTIVE _____

VERB ENDING IN "ING" _____

PLURAL NOUN _____

LANGUAGE _____

PART OF THE BODY _____

ADJECTIVE _____

ADJECTIVE _____

TYPE OF FOOD (PLURAL) _____

SILLY WORD (PLURAL) _____

VERB ENDING IN "ING" _____

MAD LIBS®
LETTER TO A FRIEND BACK HOME

Dear _____,
<u>PERSON IN ROOM</u>

Well, here we are at the _____ Seaside Hotel in (the)
<u>ADJECTIVE</u>

_____. The weather is _____ and the temperature
<u>A PLACE</u>   <u>ADJECTIVE</u>

is _____ degrees. Our hotel room looks out onto a garden filled
<u>NUMBER</u>

with _____ trees and tropical _____. The
<u>TYPE OF FOOD</u>   <u>PLURAL NOUN</u>

natives are all _____ and spend their time _____
<u>ADJECTIVE</u>   <u>VERB ENDING IN "ING"</u>

and riding their _____ through the streets. Most of them speak
<u>PLURAL NOUN</u>

_____, but I can communicate with them by making signs with
<u>LANGUAGE</u>

my _____. The local food is really _____. Mostly
<u>PART OF THE BODY</u>   <u>ADJECTIVE</u>

they eat _____ burritos and refried _____.
<u>ADJECTIVE</u>   <u>TYPE OF FOOD (PLURAL)</u>

Our hotel costs only a hundred _____ a day. We are going to
<u>SILLY WORD (PLURAL)</u>

spend the week _____ and then come home. Wish you
<u>VERB ENDING IN "ING"</u>

were here.

MAD LIBS® is fun to play with friends, but you can also play it by yourself! To begin with, DO NOT look at the story on the page below. Fill in the blanks on this page with the words called for. Then, using the words you have selected, fill in the blank spaces in the story.

Now you've created your own hilarious MAD LIBS® game!

MEDICAL DRAMA

PERSON IN ROOM _____

PERSON IN ROOM _____

PERSON IN ROOM (MALE) _____

PART OF THE BODY _____

NOUN _____

ADVERB _____

PART OF THE BODY _____

NOUN _____

VERB ENDING IN "S" _____

NOUN _____

NOUN _____

NOUN _____

NOUN _____

NOUN _____

ADJECTIVE _____

MAD LIBS®
MEDICAL DRAMA

Starring _____, _____, and _____.
            PERSON IN ROOM   PERSON IN ROOM   PERSON IN ROOM (MALE)

NURSE: Thank goodness you're here, doctor. A patient was just brought in with

a badly bruised _____ and a ruptured _____.
                    PART OF THE BODY   NOUN

Unfortunately, Dr. Smith plans to operate _____.
                                                ADVERB

DOCTOR: We can't let him! Look at the way his _____
                                                    PART OF THE BODY

is shaking.

NURSE: Uh-oh, he's putting a mask over his _____!
                                                NOUN

Doctor, stop him before he _____ somebody.
                              VERB ENDING IN "S"

DOCTOR: Smith, you can't operate on this _____! I forbid it.
                                            NOUN

SMITH: How dare you say that to me? I'm your mentor. You're like a/an

_____ to me.
    NOUN

DOCTOR: And you're like a/an _____ to me, but I can't risk
                                NOUN

the wrath of a/an _____ to satisfy your ego. Look in the mirror.
                      NOUN

Would you trust that _____ to remove a/an _____ nail?
                          NOUN   ADJECTIVE

MAD LIBS® is fun to play with friends, but you can also play it by yourself! To begin with, DO NOT look at the story on the page below. Fill in the blanks on this page with the words called for. Then, using the words you have selected, fill in the blank spaces in the story.

Now you've created your own hilarious MAD LIBS® game!

A SPOOKY, SCARY, SLIMY STORY

ADJECTIVE _____

VERB ENDING IN "ING" _____

NOUN _____

PLURAL NOUN _____

PART OF THE BODY _____

ADJECTIVE _____

ADJECTIVE _____

NOUN _____

ADVERB _____

NOUN _____

ADJECTIVE _____

ADJECTIVE _____

VERB _____

NOUN _____

NOUN _____

ADJECTIVE _____

MAD LIBS®
A SPOOKY, SCARY, SLIMY STORY

It was a dark and _____ night. The wind was _____
_____ADJECTIVE_____   _____VERB ENDING IN "ING"_____

through the trees, and off in the distance wolves were howling at the

_____. I wanted to get home as fast as my _____
_____NOUN_____   _____PLURAL NOUN_____

could carry me. My _____ was pounding, and my breath was
_____PART OF THE BODY_____

coming in _____ gasps. Suddenly, I felt the _____
_____ADJECTIVE_____   _____ADJECTIVE_____

hand of a/an _____ touch my neck, and I screamed
_____NOUN_____

_____. The monster lifted me off the _____ and
_____ADVERB_____   _____NOUN_____

threw me onto the _____ ground. Then, with his _____
_____ADJECTIVE_____   _____ADJECTIVE_____

hands, he tried to _____ the _____ out of me.
_____VERB_____   _____NOUN_____

I screamed so loudly, I woke up every _____ in the forest. My
_____NOUN_____

scream awakened me, too—I was having a/an _____ nightmare.
_____ADJECTIVE_____

MAD LIBS® is fun to play with friends, but you can also play it by yourself! To begin with, DO NOT look at the story on the page below. Fill in the blanks on this page with the words called for. Then, using the words you have selected, fill in the blank spaces in the story.

Now you've created your own hilarious MAD LIBS® game!

ADVERTISEMENT

NOUN _____

ADJECTIVE _____

NOUN _____

VERB ENDING IN "ING" _____

ADJECTIVE _____

NOUN _____

ADJECTIVE _____

ADJECTIVE _____

NOUN _____

PLURAL NOUN _____

NOUN _____

PLURAL NOUN _____

ADJECTIVE _____

PLURAL NOUN _____

ADJECTIVE _____

NOUN _____

NOUN _____

PART OF THE BODY _____

NOUN _____

MAD LIBS®
ADVERTISEMENT

Look at yourself in the _____. What does your _____
                              NOUN   ADJECTIVE

face tell you? Right! It's time to treat your tired _____ to an ocean-
                                                          NOUN

_____ cruise. So do it! Sail in style on a/an _____
VERB ENDING IN "ING"   ADJECTIVE

luxury _____. Whether it's the _____ spaciousness
            NOUN   ADJECTIVE

of our staterooms or the _____ elegance of our salons,
                              ADJECTIVE

everything is fit for a/an _____. Our ships are skippered by
                              NOUN

Norwegian _____, whose ancestors, dating back to the ninth
                PLURAL NOUN

_____, were seafaring _____. Europe's most
        NOUN   PLURAL NOUN

_____ chefs prepare your culinary _____. Our
    ADJECTIVE   PLURAL NOUN

pastry chef creates _____ desserts that melt in your
                          ADJECTIVE

_____. Our dashing waiters are at your _____
        NOUN   NOUN

before you can raise a/an _____. Don't delay—plan to sail today.
                              PART OF THE BODY

Now look in the mirror. How about that smiling _____?
                                                      NOUN

MAD LIBS® is fun to play with friends, but you can also play it by yourself! To begin with, DO NOT look at the story on the page below. Fill in the blanks on this page with the words called for. Then, using the words you have selected, fill in the blank spaces in the story.

Now you've created your own hilarious MAD LIBS® game!

A CASE OF PUPPY LOVE

NOUN _____

PERSON IN ROOM (MALE) _____

PERSON IN ROOM (MALE) _____

ADJECTIVE _____

NOUN _____

NOUN _____

NUMBER _____

NOUN _____

PLURAL NOUN _____

PART OF THE BODY _____

NOUN _____

VERB ENDING IN "ING" _____

ADJECTIVE _____

NOUN _____

NOUN _____

NOUN _____

NOUN _____

ADJECTIVE _____

NOUN _____

PLURAL NOUN _____

MAD LIBS®
A CASE OF PUPPY LOVE

(A telephone monologue to be read by a/an _____ in pajamas.)
NOUN

Hi, _____. It's me, _____. I hope I didn't wake
PERSON IN ROOM (MALE)   PERSON IN ROOM (MALE)

you from a/an _____ sleep. Sure, I know what _____
ADJECTIVE   NOUN

it is. I have a digital _____ right by my bed. It's _____ A.M.
NOUN   NUMBER

But when I sleep over at your house, this is always the time you get up to go to

the _____. I can't go to sleep. I haven't even *been* asleep. I haven't
NOUN

closed my _____ even once. Every time my _____
PLURAL NOUN   PART OF THE BODY

hits the _____ I start tossing and _____.
NOUN   VERB ENDING IN "ING"

Nothing's the matter—I just have _____ news, and I have to
ADJECTIVE

tell someone: My mom changed her _____ and said I can have
NOUN

a puppy, provided I feed and _____-break it. I want you to go
NOUN

with me to the shelter and pick out a/an _____. I don't care
NOUN

what breed. It can be a Cocker _____ or a/an _____
NOUN   ADJECTIVE

Retriever or even a German _____. I'll see you first thing in the
NOUN

morning. Go back to sleep. Try counting _____.
PLURAL NOUN

MAD LIBS® is fun to play with friends, but you can also play it by yourself! To begin with, DO NOT look at the story on the page below. Fill in the blanks on this page with the words called for. Then, using the words you have selected, fill in the blank spaces in the story.

Now you've created your own hilarious MAD LIBS® game!

CAR OF THE YEAR

LAST NAME OF PERSON IN ROOM _____

NOUN _____

NOUN _____

PLURAL NOUN _____

PLURAL NOUN _____

PLURAL NOUN _____

PLURAL NOUN _____

TYPE OF LIQUID _____

NOUN _____

VERB _____

SAME LAST NAME _____

PART OF THE BODY (PLURAL) _____

NOUN _____

ADJECTIVE _____

NOUN _____

EXCLAMATION _____

MAD LIBS®
CAR OF THE YEAR

It's here, the all-new _____: the most luxurious
                        LAST NAME OF PERSON IN ROOM

_____ you'll ever drive! It's the only four-door _____
      NOUN   NOUN

that comes equipped with dual air _____, power _____,
                                   PLURAL NOUN   PLURAL NOUN

and contoured, plush leather _____. And, believe it or
                              PLURAL NOUN

not, it is the only car in its class that can go up to a hundred thousand

_____ without needing a/an _____ change
    PLURAL NOUN   TYPE OF LIQUID

or a/an _____ tune-up. Run, do not _____,
             NOUN   VERB

to your nearest _____ dealer and feast your
                        SAME LAST NAME

_____ on the car that *Motor* _____
 PART OF THE BODY (PLURAL)   NOUN

magazine calls the _____ _____ of the year.
                        ADJECTIVE   NOUN

As always, we save the best for last: When you see the sticker price, you'll be sure

to shout, "_____!"
           EXCLAMATION

MAD LIBS® is fun to play with friends, but you can also play it by yourself! To begin with, DO NOT look at the story on the page below. Fill in the blanks on this page with the words called for. Then, using the words you have selected, fill in the blank spaces in the story.

Now you've created your own hilarious MAD LIBS® game!

A TYPICAL HISTORY TEST

NOUN _____

PLURAL NOUN _____

A PLACE _____

NOUN _____

PLURAL NOUN _____

PLURAL NOUN _____

FOREIGN COUNTRY _____

NOUN _____

ADJECTIVE _____

PERSON IN ROOM (MALE) _____

CELEBRITY (MALE) _____

CELEBRITY (MALE) _____

VERB ENDING IN "ING" _____

CELEBRITY (MALE) _____

PLURAL NOUN _____

CELEBRITY (FEMALE) _____

MAD LIBS®
A TYPICAL HISTORY TEST

Instructions: When the _____ *rings, unfold your papers and*
                          NOUN

answer the following _____.
                         PLURAL NOUN

1. What general won the Battle of (the) _____?
                                          A PLACE

2. Which American _____ said, "Give me liberty or give me
                       NOUN

   _____"?
      PLURAL NOUN

3. Who was the first president of the United _____ of
                                                PLURAL NOUN

   _____?
     FOREIGN COUNTRY

4. Why did Benjamin Franklin fly a/an _____ during a thunderstorm?
                                          NOUN

5. Who made the first _____ flag?
                            ADJECTIVE

ANSWERS TO TEST:

1. _____.
     PERSON IN ROOM (MALE)

2. _____, when he was executed by _____
       CELEBRITY (MALE)   CELEBRITY (MALE)

   for _____.
         VERB ENDING IN "ING"

3. _____.
     CELEBRITY (MALE)

4. He was discovering _____.
                           PLURAL NOUN

5. _____.
     CELEBRITY (FEMALE)

MAD LIBS® is fun to play with friends, but you can also play it by yourself! To begin with, DO NOT look at the story on the page below. Fill in the blanks on this page with the words called for. Then, using the words you have selected, fill in the blank spaces in the story.

Now you've created your own hilarious MAD LIBS® game!

MY MOST EMBARRASSING MOMENT

PERSON IN ROOM _____

GEOGRAPHICAL LOCATION _____

ADJECTIVE _____

NOUN _____

NOUN _____

NOUN _____

PART OF THE BODY _____

PART OF THE BODY _____

PART OF THE BODY _____

ADJECTIVE _____

NOUN _____

ADJECTIVE _____

NOUN _____

NOUN _____

MAD LIBS®
MY MOST EMBARRASSING MOMENT

By _____
PERSON IN ROOM

My most embarrassing moment happened when I got on a bus to go to

_____. The bus was very _____, so I stood
GEOGRAPHICAL LOCATION   ADJECTIVE

up and held on to a/an _____. At the next stop, I saw a/an
NOUN

_____ get up, and I ran over to grab his _____, but
NOUN   NOUN

I accidentally jabbed my _____ into his _____
PART OF THE BODY   PART OF THE BODY

and broke his _____. And then as I was apologizing,
PART OF THE BODY

the bus came to a/an _____ stop, which caused me to drop my
ADJECTIVE

_____ and fall on top of a/an _____ lady who was
NOUN   ADJECTIVE

carrying a/an _____ on her lap. Believe me, my _____
NOUN   NOUN

was red that day!

MAD LIBS® is fun to play with friends, but you can also play it by yourself! To begin with, DO NOT look at the story on the page below. Fill in the blanks on this page with the words called for. Then, using the words you have selected, fill in the blank spaces in the story.

Now you've created your own hilarious MAD LIBS® game!

A VISIT TO THE DENTIST

PLURAL NOUN _____

LAST NAME OF PERSON IN ROOM _____

ADJECTIVE _____

NOUN _____

NOUN _____

PART OF THE BODY _____

PART OF THE BODY _____

PLURAL NOUN _____

NOUN _____

NOUN _____

EXCLAMATION _____

NOUN _____

NOUN _____

NOUN _____

VERB _____

NOUN _____

ADJECTIVE _____

NOUN _____

MAD LIBS®
A VISIT TO THE DENTIST

A one-act play to be performed by two _____ *in this room.*
PLURAL NOUN

PATIENT: Thank you very much for seeing me, Dr. _____,
LAST NAME OF PERSON IN ROOM

especially on such _____ notice.
ADJECTIVE

DENTIST: What is your problem, young _____?
NOUN

PATIENT: I have a pain in my upper _____, which is giving
NOUN

me a severe _____-ache.
PART OF THE BODY

DENTIST: Let me take a look. Open your _____ wide. Good.
PART OF THE BODY

Now I'm going to tap your _____ with my _____.
PLURAL NOUN   NOUN

PATIENT: Shouldn't you give me a/an _____ killer?
NOUN

DENTIST: It's not necessary yet. _____! I think I see a/an
EXCLAMATION

_____ in your upper _____.
NOUN   NOUN

PATIENT: Are you going to pull my _____ out?
NOUN

DENTIST: No. I'm going to _____ your tooth and put in a
VERB

temporary _____.
NOUN

PATIENT: When do I come back for the _____ filling?
ADJECTIVE

DENTIST: A day after I wash your _____.
NOUN

MAD LIBS® is fun to play with friends, but you can also play it by yourself! To begin with, DO NOT look at the story on the page below. Fill in the blanks on this page with the words called for. Then, using the words you have selected, fill in the blank spaces in the story.

Now you've created your own hilarious MAD LIBS® game!

MOON FACTS

ADJECTIVE _____

NOUN _____

NOUN _____

ADJECTIVE _____

PLURAL NOUN _____

VERB ENDING IN "S" _____

NUMBER _____

NOUN _____

SAME NOUN _____

PERSON IN ROOM _____

PERSON IN ROOM _____

NOUN _____

PLURAL NOUN _____

PART OF THE BODY _____

PLURAL NOUN _____

ADJECTIVE _____

NOUN _____

MAD LIBS®
MOON FACTS

1. Even though the moon first appears as a/an _____ slice of
   ADJECTIVE

   light and finally becomes a full _____, it doesn't change its
   NOUN

   _____. The moon looks as different as the _____
   NOUN   ADJECTIVE

   sun illuminates its different _____.
   PLURAL NOUN

2. The moon _____ around the earth once every
   VERB ENDING IN "S"

   _____ days.
   NUMBER

3. If the moon were to be seen next to the earth it would look like a tennis

   _____ next to a bowling _____.
   NOUN   SAME NOUN

4. In 1969, _____ and _____, from the
   PERSON IN ROOM   PERSON IN ROOM

   Apollo _____, were the first human _____ to set
   NOUN   PLURAL NOUN

   _____ on the moon. Many historians and _____
   PART OF THE BODY   PLURAL NOUN

   believe this to be the most _____ achievement in the
   ADJECTIVE

   history of the _____.
   NOUN

MAD LIBS® is fun to play with friends, but you can also play it by yourself! To begin with, DO NOT look at the story on the page below. Fill in the blanks on this page with the words called for. Then, using the words you have selected, fill in the blank spaces in the story.

Now you've created your own hilarious MAD LIBS® game!

THE THREE MUSKETEERS

ADJECTIVE _____

PLURAL NOUN _____

ADJECTIVE _____

NOUN _____

ADJECTIVE _____

NOUN _____

NOUN _____

PLURAL NOUN _____

NOUN _____

PERSON IN ROOM _____

PLURAL NOUN _____

ADJECTIVE _____

NOUN _____

NOUN _____

PLURAL NOUN _____

NOUN _____

MAD LIBS®
THE THREE MUSKETEERS

There is no more rousing story in _____ literature than
                                        ADJECTIVE

The Three _____. This _____ romance, by
                PLURAL NOUN   ADJECTIVE

the great French _____ Alexandre Dumas, tells the story of
                        NOUN

d'Artagnan, a/an _____ young _____ who
                        ADJECTIVE   NOUN

arrives in seventeenth-century Paris riding a/an _____ with
                                                        NOUN

only three _____ in his pocket. Determined to be in the service
                PLURAL NOUN

of the _____ who rules all of France, he duels with Athos,
                NOUN

Porthos, and _____, three of the king's best _____.
                PERSON IN ROOM   PLURAL NOUN

Eventually, these swordsmen and d'Artagnan save their _____
                                                                ADJECTIVE

king from being overthrown and losing his _____. Over the
                                                    NOUN

years, *The Three Musketeers* has been made into a stage _____,
                                                                    NOUN

two motion _____, and, most recently, a Broadway
                PLURAL NOUN

_____.
        NOUN

MAD LIBS® is fun to play with friends, but you can also play it by yourself! To begin with, DO NOT look at the story on the page below. Fill in the blanks on this page with the words called for. Then, using the words you have selected, fill in the blank spaces in the story.

Now you've created your own hilarious MAD LIBS® game!

A CHARMING STORY WITH A HAPPY ENDING

NOUN _____

ADJECTIVE _____

PLURAL NOUN _____

ADJECTIVE _____

PLURAL NOUN _____

ADJECTIVE _____

PLURAL NOUN _____

EXCLAMATION _____

VERB _____

VERB _____

NOUN _____

NOUN _____

ADJECTIVE _____

VERB (PAST TENSE) _____

ADJECTIVE _____

NOUN _____

MAD LIBS®

A CHARMING STORY WITH A HAPPY ENDING

Once upon a/an _____, there were three little pigs. The first
                        NOUN

little pig was very _____, and he built a house for himself out
                        ADJECTIVE

of _____. The second little pig was _____,
      PLURAL NOUN   ADJECTIVE

and he built a house out of _____. But the third little pig
                                PLURAL NOUN

was very _____, and he built his house out of genuine
              ADJECTIVE

_____. Well, one day, a mean old wolf came along and saw the
   PLURAL NOUN

houses. "_____!" he said. "I'll _____ and I'll
            EXCLAMATION   VERB

_____ and I'll blow your house down." And he blew down the
   VERB

first little pig's _____ and the second little pig's _____.
                      NOUN   NOUN

The two little pigs ran to the third pig's house. Thereupon, the wolf began

blowing, but he couldn't blow down the third little pig's _____
                                                              ADJECTIVE

house. So he _____ off into the forest, and the three little
                VERB (PAST TENSE)

_____ pigs moved to Chicago and went into the _____
   ADJECTIVE   NOUN

business.

MAD LIBS® is fun to play with friends, but you can also play it by yourself! To begin with, DO NOT look at the story on the page below. Fill in the blanks on this page with the words called for. Then, using the words you have selected, fill in the blank spaces in the story.

Now you've created your own hilarious MAD LIBS® game!

THE GARAGE BAND

ADJECTIVE _____

ADJECTIVE _____

VERB _____

NOUN _____

VERB ENDING IN "ING" _____

NOUN _____

ADJECTIVE _____

PLURAL NOUN _____

ADJECTIVE _____

NOUN _____

SILLY WORD _____

PLURAL NOUN _____

ADJECTIVE _____

ADJECTIVE _____

PERSON IN ROOM _____

PERSON IN ROOM _____

PERSON IN ROOM _____

PLURAL NOUN _____

NOUN _____

NOUN _____

MAD LIBS®
THE GARAGE BAND

Dad plays a/an _____ piano. A/An _____ musician,
ADJECTIVE   ADJECTIVE

he's equally at home with rock 'n' _____ as he is with classical
VERB

_____. Mom has a remarkable _____
NOUN   VERB ENDING IN "ING"

voice and was the lead _____ in her college choir. She never
NOUN

failed to hit a/an _____ note. Music flows through our family's
ADJECTIVE

_____—with the exception of Cousin Joel, who doesn't have
PLURAL NOUN

a/an _____ ear for music and can't carry a/an _____.
ADJECTIVE   NOUN

But believe it or not, he just formed a garage band. They are called the

_____ _____. Fortunately, Joel's only the
SILLY WORD   PLURAL NOUN

_____ manager. Three of our other cousins make up the
ADJECTIVE

_____ band. _____ plays guitar, _____
ADJECTIVE   PERSON IN ROOM   PERSON IN ROOM

plays bass, and _____ plays the _____. It's been
PERSON IN ROOM   PLURAL NOUN

only three weeks since they got together and they've already been booked—at

the local police _____ for disturbing the _____.
NOUN   NOUN

MAD LIBS® is fun to play with friends, but you can also play it by yourself! To begin with, DO NOT look at the story on the page below. Fill in the blanks on this page with the words called for. Then, using the words you have selected, fill in the blank spaces in the story.

Now you've created your own hilarious MAD LIBS® game!

LETTER FROM A MARTIAN

NOUN _____

NOUN _____

ADJECTIVE _____

VERB _____

ADJECTIVE _____

PERSON IN ROOM _____

ADJECTIVE _____

VERB _____

VERB ENDING IN "ING" _____

NOUN _____

PLURAL NOUN _____

NOUN _____

MAD LIBS®
LETTER FROM A MARTIAN

Dear Earthling,

I am a teenage _____ who lives in a two-story _____
                    NOUN   NOUN

on Mars. I will put this letter in a/an _____ bottle and
                                        ADJECTIVE

_____ it into space and hope that it gets to Earth.
      VERB

Of course, on Mars we call your _____ planet _____.
                                 ADJECTIVE   PERSON IN ROOM

We know that it is inhabited by _____ little pink men and
                                     ADJECTIVE

women, but I would like to hear from you anyway. Tell me, how do you people

_____ your food?
      VERB

We do it by _____ rapidly.
            VERB ENDING IN "ING"

I hope you will be able to visit me someday. You could stay in our

_____ and eat _____ just like we do, and you
      NOUN   PLURAL NOUN

could play with my pet _____.
                          NOUN

MAD LIBS® is fun to play with friends, but you can also play it by yourself! To begin with, DO NOT look at the story on the page below. Fill in the blanks on this page with the words called for. Then, using the words you have selected, fill in the blank spaces in the story.

Now you've created your own hilarious MAD LIBS® game!

DOWNHILL SKI RACE

PLURAL NOUN _____

VERB _____

NOUN _____

ADJECTIVE _____

VERB ENDING IN "ING" _____

NOUN _____

PLURAL NOUN _____

NOUN _____

PART OF THE BODY _____

PLURAL NOUN _____

ADJECTIVE _____

PLURAL NOUN _____

NOUN _____

NOUN _____

NOUN _____

MAD LIBS®
DOWNHILL SKI RACE

From the moment the downhill _____ leave the gates until
PLURAL NOUN

the second they _____ across the finish line, the ski race is
VERB

a/an _____-pounding experience! The skiers must navigate
NOUN

a/an _____, demanding course, _____ over
ADJECTIVE   VERB ENDING IN "ING"

giant mounds of _____ known as "moguls" and maneuvering
NOUN

around plastic _____ planted in the snow, which create a more
PLURAL NOUN

challenging _____. If that isn't tough enough, the racers have
NOUN

to combat the elements—the _____-chilling cold, the blinding
PART OF THE BODY

snow _____, and the _____ winds racing up
PLURAL NOUN   ADJECTIVE

to one hundred _____ per hour. Only the results of a downhill
PLURAL NOUN

_____ are predictable. It seems that, year after year, the same
NOUN

team wins this _____. Must be something in its _____!
NOUN   NOUN

MAD LIBS® is fun to play with friends, but you can also play it by yourself! To begin with, DO NOT look at the story on the page below. Fill in the blanks on this page with the words called for. Then, using the words you have selected, fill in the blank spaces in the story.

Now you've created your own hilarious MAD LIBS® game!

THE GETTYSBURG ADDRESS

PLURAL NOUN _____

NOUN _____

ADJECTIVE _____

PLURAL NOUN _____

ADJECTIVE _____

NOUN _____

SAME NOUN _____

ADJECTIVE _____

CELEBRITY _____

PLURAL NOUN _____

SAME PLURAL NOUN _____

SAME PLURAL NOUN _____

NOUN _____

MAD LIBS®
THE GETTYSBURG ADDRESS

Fourscore and seven years ago, our _____ brought forth on this
                                        PLURAL NOUN

_____ a/an _____ nation, conceived in liberty
        NOUN   ADJECTIVE

and dedicated to the proposition that all _____ are created
                                              PLURAL NOUN

_____. Now we are engaged in a great civil war, testing
    ADJECTIVE

whether that _____ or any _____ so conceived
                    NOUN   SAME NOUN

and so dedicated, can long endure. It is rather for us to be here dedicated to the

_____ task remaining before us . . . that this nation, under
    ADJECTIVE

_____, shall have a new birth of freedom, and that government of the
  CELEBRITY

_____, by the _____, for the _____
  PLURAL NOUN   SAME PLURAL NOUN   SAME PLURAL NOUN

shall not perish from the _____.
                              NOUN

MAD LIBS® is fun to play with friends, but you can also play it by yourself! To begin with, DO NOT look at the story on the page below. Fill in the blanks on this page with the words called for. Then, using the words you have selected, fill in the blank spaces in the story.

Now you've created your own hilarious MAD LIBS® game!

SOME PHYSICAL LAWS ALL SHOULD KNOW

TYPE OF GAS_____

VERB _____

NOUN _____

NOUN _____

PLURAL NOUN_____

NUMBER _____

PLURAL NOUN_____

SILLY WORD _____

TYPE OF LIQUID_____

NOUN _____

DIRECTION_____

DIRECTION_____

MAD LIBS®

SOME PHYSICAL LAWS ALL SHOULD KNOW

1. If you apply heat to _____, it will _____.
   TYPE OF GAS   VERB

2. Water always seeks its own _____.
   NOUN

3. In a right triangle, the square of the _____ is equal to the
   NOUN

   sum of the squares of the other two _____.
   PLURAL NOUN

4. Sound travels through air at the rate of _____ _____
   NUMBER   PLURAL NOUN

   per second.

5. Weight: Sixteen ounces equals one _____.
   SILLY WORD

6. If an object is floating in _____, it displaces its own
   TYPE OF LIQUID

   _____.
   NOUN

7. Everything that goes _____ must come _____.
   DIRECTION   DIRECTION

MAD LIBS® is fun to play with friends, but you can also play it by yourself! To begin with, DO NOT look at the story on the page below. Fill in the blanks on this page with the words called for. Then, using the words you have selected, fill in the blank spaces in the story.

Now you've created your own hilarious MAD LIBS® game!

THE BLOB

SOMETHING ALIVE (PLURAL)_____

COLOR _____

TYPE OF ICKY FOOD_____

ADJECTIVE _____

CITY_____

CELEBRITY (MALE) _____

TYPE OF LIQUID _____

TYPE OF FOOD (PLURAL) _____

VERB ENDING IN "ING"_____

NOUN _____

ANIMAL_____

ADVERB _____

EXCLAMATION _____

PART OF THE BODY _____

PLURAL NOUN_____

CELEBRITY (FEMALE) _____

PLURAL NOUN_____

MAD LIBS®
THE BLOB

The Blob is one of those movies Hollywood _____ keep
SOMETHING ALIVE (PLURAL)

remaking every few years. The main character is a huge _____
COLOR

lump of pulsating _____ that wants to become the first
TYPE OF ICKY FOOD

_____ mayor of the city of _____. It was
ADJECTIVE   CITY

created by a scientist, played by _____. The scientist
CELEBRITY (MALE)

accidentally dropped some _____ into a dish full of
TYPE OF LIQUID

_____. The food immediately started _____
TYPE OF FOOD (PLURAL)   VERB ENDING IN "ING"

and eventually grew to be the size of a/an _____. The Blob eats
NOUN

up the scientist and his favorite _____, and begins to roll
ANIMAL

_____ down the street. When people see it, they say,
ADVERB

"_____!" But the Blob just opens its _____
EXCLAMATION   PART OF THE BODY

and swallows them, along with any _____ that are in the
PLURAL NOUN

neighborhood. Finally, it gets to the power company, where the heroine, played

by _____, manages to kill it with one hundred thousand
CELEBRITY (FEMALE)

_____.
PLURAL NOUN

MAD LIBS® is fun to play with friends, but you can also play it by yourself! To begin with, DO NOT look at the story on the page below. Fill in the blanks on this page with the words called for. Then, using the words you have selected, fill in the blank spaces in the story.

Now you've created your own hilarious MAD LIBS® game!

SWIMMING

PLURAL NOUN _____

ADJECTIVE _____

VERB _____

NOUN _____

PART OF THE BODY _____

VERB _____

ADJECTIVE _____

ADJECTIVE _____

VERB _____

ADJECTIVE _____

NOUN _____

NOUN _____

MAD LIBS®
SWIMMING

Many Americans have swimming _____ in their backyards
                                    PLURAL NOUN

and learn to swim at a very _____ age. Learning to swim is
                                    ADJECTIVE

easier than learning to _____ or read a/an _____.
                              VERB   NOUN

First, you float on your _____ until you're able to _____
                         PART OF THE BODY   VERB

across the pool. If you work hard, in no time at all you can master the

_____ crawl and the _____ stroke,
            ADJECTIVE   ADJECTIVE

and you can even _____ underwater. Remember, with
                         VERB

lots of practice, you can become a/an _____ champion
                                            ADJECTIVE

_____ on the U.S. Olympic _____.
        NOUN   NOUN

MAD LIBS® is fun to play with friends, but you can also play it by yourself! To begin with, DO NOT look at the story on the page below. Fill in the blanks on this page with the words called for. Then, using the words you have selected, fill in the blank spaces in the story.

Now you've created your own hilarious MAD LIBS® game!

DINOSAURS FROM A TO Z

ADJECTIVE _____

ADVERB _____

ADJECTIVE _____

ADJECTIVE _____

PLURAL NOUN _____

PLURAL NOUN _____

PLURAL NOUN _____

PLURAL NOUN _____

NUMBER _____

NOUN _____

PLURAL NOUN _____

ADJECTIVE _____

PLURAL NOUN _____

NOUN _____

ADJECTIVE _____

PLURAL NOUN _____

ADJECTIVE _____

ADJECTIVE _____

ADJECTIVE _____

TYPE OF VEGETABLE _____

MAD LIBS®
DINOSAURS FROM A TO Z

To make it easier to learn the _____ names of dinosaurs, we will
                                    ADJECTIVE

spell them out _____ for you.
                  ADVERB

ACANTHOPHOLIS (a-can-THAW-pho-lis): This creature carried its _____
                                                                    ADJECTIVE

body on _____ legs. Its diet probably consisted of _____
          ADJECTIVE   PLURAL NOUN

and perhaps even some small _____.
                              PLURAL NOUN

HYPSILOPHODON (hyp-sil-AW-pho-don): It is thought that this dinosaur climbed

_____, because the toes on its _____ pointed
   PLURAL NOUN   PLURAL NOUN

backward. It lived for more than _____ years, longer than any
                                    NUMBER

other _____ known to _____.
         NOUN   PLURAL NOUN

STEGOSAURUS (steg-uh-SAWR-us): This dinosaur had a/an _____
                                                           ADJECTIVE

arrangement of huge _____ on its neck, back, and _____. In
                       PLURAL NOUN   NOUN

battle, this creature would swing its _____ tail at its _____.
                                         ADJECTIVE   PLURAL NOUN

ZEPHYROSAURUS (zeph-y-ro-SAWR-us): This creature was known as the

_____ lizard. Most of these giants had a/an _____
   ADJECTIVE   ADJECTIVE

neck with a/an _____ head and a/an _____-
                  ADJECTIVE   TYPE OF VEGETABLE

sized brain.

MAD LIBS® is fun to play with friends, but you can also play it by yourself! To begin with, DO NOT look at the story on the page below. Fill in the blanks on this page with the words called for. Then, using the words you have selected, fill in the blank spaces in the story.

Now you've created your own hilarious MAD LIBS® game!

BEAUTY ADVICE

ADJECTIVE _____

ADJECTIVE _____

PART OF THE BODY _____

NOUN _____

TYPE OF CONTAINER _____

TYPE OF LIQUID_____

PLURAL NOUN_____

PLURAL NOUN_____

ADJECTIVE _____

ADJECTIVE _____

NOUN _____

ADJECTIVE _____

ADJECTIVE _____

ADJECTIVE _____

ADVERB _____

ADJECTIVE _____

PERSON IN ROOM _____

MAD LIBS®
BEAUTY ADVICE

If your skin is _____ or _____, you can cure
                        ADJECTIVE   ADJECTIVE

this condition with the following regimen. Every morning, before washing your

_____, massage it gently with a/an _____
     PART OF THE BODY   NOUN

that has been soaked overnight in a/an _____ full of warm
                                                TYPE OF CONTAINER

_____. Then mix together some _____ and
     TYPE OF LIQUID   PLURAL NOUN

some _____ until the mixture becomes _____,
           PLURAL NOUN   ADJECTIVE

and pat it onto your _____ face for five minutes. Then remove it
                                  ADJECTIVE

using a/an _____, and wash your face with _____
                    NOUN   ADJECTIVE

water. Do not omit this _____ step, or your skin will become
                                      ADJECTIVE

_____. Do this _____ every day, and soon you
        ADJECTIVE   ADVERB

will be as _____ as _____.
                    ADJECTIVE   PERSON IN ROOM

MAD LIBS® is fun to play with friends, but you can also play it by yourself! To begin with, DO NOT look at the story on the page below. Fill in the blanks on this page with the words called for. Then, using the words you have selected, fill in the blank spaces in the story.

Now you've created your own hilarious MAD LIBS® game!

SCIENCE-FICTION STORY

NOUN _____

GEOGRAPHICAL LOCATION _____

NUMBER _____

ADVERB _____

SILLY WORD _____

NOUN _____

SILLY WORD _____

VERB (PAST TENSE) _____

SILLY WORD _____

EXCLAMATION _____

SILLY WORD _____

SILLY WORD _____

SILLY WORD _____

MAD LIBS®
SCIENCE-FICTION STORY

Major Zarnak of the Intergalactic Space Patrol deactivated his hyper-

_____ overdrive and landed his spaceship on the planet
      NOUN

_____. On leaving the decompression chamber, he saw a/an
  GEOGRAPHICAL LOCATION

_____-armed monster approaching _____. He
      NUMBER   ADVERB

shouted, "_____," the galactic word for peace, but the monster
      SILLY WORD

whipped out a disintegrator _____ and tried to _____
                      NOUN   SILLY WORD

him. Major Zarnak ducked and _____ the monster with
                            VERB (PAST TENSE)

his subsonic _____. "_____!" said the mon-
           SILLY WORD   EXCLAMATION

ster, clutching his _____. "_____" replied
            SILLY WORD   SILLY WORD

Major Zarnak cleverly, and, getting into his spaceship, he zipped back to his

headquarters on the planet _____.
                      SILLY WORD

MAD LIBS® is fun to play with friends, but you can also play it by yourself! To begin with, DO NOT look at the story on the page below. Fill in the blanks on this page with the words called for. Then, using the words you have selected, fill in the blank spaces in the story.

Now you've created your own hilarious MAD LIBS® game!

KEYBOARDING TIPS

NUMBER _____

FOREIGN COUNTRY _____

ADVERB _____

VERB ENDING IN "ING" _____

PART OF THE BODY (PLURAL) _____

PLURAL NOUN _____

TYPE OF BUILDING _____

ADJECTIVE _____

PART OF THE BODY (PLURAL) _____

SAME PART OF THE BODY (PLURAL) _____

PLURAL NOUN _____

VERB ENDING IN "ING" _____

NUMBER _____

PLURAL NOUN _____

VERB _____

PLURAL NOUN _____

LANGUAGE_____

NOUN _____

MAD LIBS®
KEYBOARDING TIPS

Since you'll most likely be on your computer for _____ hours a day,
NUMBER

it's very important that you learn how to type quickly. This way, you'll be able

to finish your research project on _____ _____
FOREIGN COUNTRY   ADVERB

and amaze your friends with your _____ skills! Since my
VERB ENDING IN "ING"

_____ would never land on the _____
PART OF THE BODY (PLURAL)   PLURAL NOUN

correctly, I decided to take a keyboarding class at my local _____.
TYPE OF BUILDING

My teacher was _____! The first thing he told me to do was to
ADJECTIVE

properly position my _____ on the keyboard. Then he showed
PART OF THE BODY (PLURAL)

me how to move my _____ to be able to type actual
SAME PART OF THE BODY (PLURAL)

_____! I practiced my _____ skills every night
PLURAL NOUN   VERB ENDING IN "ING"

until I could type _____ words a minute! All of my _____
NUMBER   PLURAL NOUN

are so jealous—I _____ so fast that I am always the first one
VERB

to finish typing my _____ for _____ class. All
PLURAL NOUN   LANGUAGE

those hours of hard _____ were worth it.
NOUN

MAD LIBS® is fun to play with friends, but you can also play it by yourself! To begin with, DO NOT look at the story on the page below. Fill in the blanks on this page with the words called for. Then, using the words you have selected, fill in the blank spaces in the story.

Now you've created your own hilarious MAD LIBS® game!

ALBERT EINSTEIN

CELEBRITY (MALE) _____

CELEBRITY (FEMALE) _____

NOUN _____

PLURAL NOUN _____

ADJECTIVE _____

PLURAL NOUN _____

ADJECTIVE _____

PLURAL NOUN _____

NOUN _____

A PLACE _____

PLURAL NOUN _____

NOUN _____

OCCUPATION (PLURAL) _____

MAD LIBS®
ALBERT EINSTEIN

Albert Einstein, the son of _____ and _____,
                                CELEBRITY (MALE)   CELEBRITY (FEMALE)

was born in Ulm, Germany, in 1879. In 1902, he had a job as an assistant

_____ at the Swiss Patent Office and attended the University of
       NOUN

Zurich. There he began studying atoms, molecules, and _____.
                                                              PLURAL NOUN

He developed his famous theory of _____ relativity, which expanded
                                        ADJECTIVE

the phenomena of subatomic _____ and _____
                                PLURAL NOUN   ADJECTIVE

magnetism. In 1921, he won the Nobel Prize in _____ and was
                                                    PLURAL NOUN

director of theoretical physics at the Kaiser Wilhelm _____ in
                                                              NOUN

Berlin. In 1933, when Hitler became chancellor of (the) _____,
                                                              A PLACE

Einstein came to America to take a post at the Institute for _____
                                                                  PLURAL NOUN

in Princeton, N.J., where his theories helped America devise the first atomic

_____. There is no question about it: Einstein was one of the
       NOUN

most brilliant _____ of our time.
               OCCUPATION (PLURAL)

MAD LIBS® is fun to play with friends, but you can also play it by yourself! To begin with, DO NOT look at the story on the page below. Fill in the blanks on this page with the words called for. Then, using the words you have selected, fill in the blank spaces in the story.

Now you've created your own hilarious MAD LIBS® game!

PIRATE MAKEOVER

ADJECTIVE _____

ADJECTIVE _____

NOUN _____

PERSON IN ROOM (MALE) _____

COLOR _____

PERSON IN ROOM (FEMALE) _____

NOUN _____

NOUN _____

PLURAL NOUN _____

PART OF THE BODY _____

NOUN _____

PART OF THE BODY _____

NOUN _____

VERB ENDING IN "ING" _____

ADJECTIVE _____

PLURAL NOUN _____

ADJECTIVE _____

PLURAL NOUN _____

PLURAL NOUN _____

ADJECTIVE _____

PLURAL NOUN _____

MAD LIBS®
PIRATE MAKEOVER

So you want to be a fierce and _____ pirate captain? First you'll
ADJECTIVE

need a/an _____-sounding pirate name, such as _____
      ADJECTIVE   NOUN

_____ or _____ _____.
PERSON IN ROOM (MALE)   COLOR   PERSON IN ROOM (FEMALE)

You'll need a mascot, too, like a pet _____, or even a/an _____
                                  NOUN   NOUN

on your shoulder that says "Aye, matey" and "Shiver me _____." Then
                                                PLURAL NOUN

you'll need to get a peg _____, put a sneer on your _____,
                  PART OF THE BODY   NOUN

and wear a patch over your _____. And every pirate captain
                           PART OF THE BODY

needs a name for his or her ship. Your vessel can be called *The Dreaded*

_____ or *The* _____.You can get all your
       NOUN   VERB ENDING IN "ING"

_____ friends together to raise the _____,
   ADJECTIVE   PLURAL NOUN

swab the _____ _____, and hoist
                 ADJECTIVE   PLURAL NOUN

the skull-and-cross-_____ flag. Now you're ready to sail the
                    PLURAL NOUN

_____ seas looking for buried _____!
   ADJECTIVE   PLURAL NOUN

MAD LIBS® is fun to play with friends, but you can also play it by yourself! To begin with, DO NOT look at the story on the page below. Fill in the blanks on this page with the words called for. Then, using the words you have selected, fill in the blank spaces in the story.

Now you've created your own hilarious MAD LIBS® game!

THE TOY STORE

SILLY WORD _____

ADJECTIVE _____

NOUN _____

PLURAL NOUN _____

PLURAL NOUN _____

ADJECTIVE _____

PLURAL NOUN _____

NUMBER _____

ADJECTIVE _____

NOUN _____

ADVERB _____

ADJECTIVE _____

ADJECTIVE _____

PERSON IN ROOM (MALE) _____

NOUN _____

MAD LIBS®
THE TOY STORE

CLERK: Good day. Welcome to the _____ Toy Shop. What can I
                                        SILLY WORD

do for you?

CUSTOMER: I would like to get a/an _____ toy for my little _____.
                                          ADJECTIVE   NOUN

CLERK: Would you like some colored _____? They stick together
                                              PLURAL NOUN

so your child can make _____ out of them.
                                PLURAL NOUN

CUSTOMER: No, my son eats anything that is _____.
                                                      ADJECTIVE

CLERK: Here are some stuffed _____. They are very popular
                                      PLURAL NOUN

with _____-year-olds.
          NUMBER

CUSTOMER: My son is a very _____ child. Last Christmas he
                                      ADJECTIVE

broke the _____ we gave him.
                NOUN

CLERK: It is important that toys can be used _____. For instance,
                                                      ADVERB

this combination walkie-talkie and rubber ducky meets the _____
                                                                      ADJECTIVE

and _____ needs of children.
          ADJECTIVE

CUSTOMER: That's very nice, but I am sure little _____ would
                                                          PERSON IN ROOM (MALE)

get bored with it after a few conversations in the tub. I think I'll get him a/an

_____, as long as it is unbreakable.
    NOUN

MAD LIBS® is fun to play with friends, but you can also play it by yourself! To begin with, DO NOT look at the story on the page below. Fill in the blanks on this page with the words called for. Then, using the words you have selected, fill in the blank spaces in the story.

Now you've created your own hilarious MAD LIBS® game!

PRIME-TIME GOSSIP

NAME OF PERSON (MALE) _____

OCCUPATION_____

ADJECTIVE _____

NAME OF PERSON (FEMALE) _____

PART OF THE BODY (PLURAL) _____

ADVERB _____

ADJECTIVE _____

ADJECTIVE _____

ADJECTIVE _____

ADJECTIVE _____

NOUN _____

CELEBRITY (MALE) _____

PERSON IN ROOM (FEMALE) _____

ADJECTIVE _____

PLURAL NOUN_____

PART OF THE BODY (PLURAL) _____

PLURAL NOUN_____

MAD LIBS®
PRIME-TIME GOSSIP

Handsome _____ and his co-_____, the
____ NAME OF PERSON (MALE) ____ OCCUPATION

_____ _____, raised _____
ADJECTIVE NAME OF PERSON (FEMALE) PART OF THE BODY (PLURAL)

when they were seen kissing _____ at the screening of their
ADVERB

_____ TV movie. The _____ couple deny it's a
ADJECTIVE ADJECTIVE

romance; they say they are just _____ friends.
ADJECTIVE

Here's another _____ tidbit: Love must be in the _____.
ADJECTIVE NOUN

_____ and _____, who had only
CELEBRITY (MALE) PERSON IN ROOM (FEMALE)

_____ words for each other last week, were seen holding
ADJECTIVE

_____ and whispering in each other's _____ at
PLURAL NOUN PART OF THE BODY (PLURAL)

this week's benefit for adopted _____.
PLURAL NOUN

MAD LIBS® is fun to play with friends, but you can also play it by yourself! To begin with, DO NOT look at the story on the page below. Fill in the blanks on this page with the words called for. Then, using the words you have selected, fill in the blank spaces in the story.

Now you've created your own hilarious MAD LIBS® game!

1-800-PSYCHIC

PLURAL NOUN _____

ADJECTIVE _____

NOUN _____

VERB ENDING IN "ING" _____

NOUN _____

NOUN _____

NOUN _____

ADJECTIVE _____

NOUN _____

ADJECTIVE _____

PLURAL NOUN _____

ADJECTIVE _____

PLURAL NOUN _____

MAD LIBS®
1-800-PSYCHIC

Psychics are _____ who are sensitive to the supernatural forces
                PLURAL NOUN

happening in this _____ world. It is believed that psychics can
                    ADJECTIVE

predict such things as the name of the _____ you are going
                                         NOUN

to marry or what your mom is _____ for dinner. If you want
                              VERB ENDING IN "ING"

to talk to a dead _____ or a dearly departed _____,
                    NOUN   NOUN

a psychic can arrange a séance. Everyone sits around a/an _____
                                                            NOUN

in a/an _____ room as the psychic goes into a/an _____
          ADJECTIVE   NOUN

and contacts the spirit of your _____ relative. Psychics also use
                                  ADJECTIVE

their abilities to help police catch _____. Today you can watch
                                      PLURAL NOUN

psychics on _____ television and call in for information that will
              ADJECTIVE

help you solve your _____.
                     PLURAL NOUN

MAD LIBS® is fun to play with friends, but you can also play it by yourself! To begin with, DO NOT look at the story on the page below. Fill in the blanks on this page with the words called for. Then, using the words you have selected, fill in the blank spaces in the story.

Now you've created your own hilarious MAD LIBS® game!

CANOEING

FOREIGN WORD _____

NUMBER _____

ADJECTIVE _____

ADJECTIVE _____

NOUN _____

PLURAL NOUN _____

ADJECTIVE _____

NOUN _____

TYPE OF LIQUID _____

VERB _____

NOUN _____

PLURAL NOUN _____

NOUN _____

NOUN _____

VERB (PAST TENSE) _____

VERB ENDING IN "ING" _____

ADJECTIVE _____

NOUN _____

MAD LIBS®
CANOEING

Canoe comes from the Spanish word _____. This type of vessel

was first described by Columbus in the year _____. It is a/an

_____ boat with its sides meeting in a/an _____ edge at

each _____. A canoe is moved by one or more _____.

It is important for you to learn the _____ way to paddle your

_____ before putting it in the _____. Should

your canoe overturn and you do not know how to _____, hang

on to the side of the _____, kick your _____,

and head for the safety of the _____. If you surface under the

canoe, locate the air _____, which will allow you to breathe

until you are _____. Once you have mastered the art of

_____, you can enjoy an overnight _____ trip,

which often is the highlight of the camping _____.

FOREIGN WORD

NUMBER

ADJECTIVE / ADJECTIVE

NOUN / PLURAL NOUN

ADJECTIVE

NOUN / TYPE OF LIQUID

VERB

NOUN / PLURAL NOUN

NOUN

NOUN

VERB (PAST TENSE)

VERB ENDING IN "ING" / ADJECTIVE

NOUN

MAD LIBS® is fun to play with friends, but you can also play it by yourself! To begin with, DO NOT look at the story on the page below. Fill in the blanks on this page with the words called for. Then, using the words you have selected, fill in the blank spaces in the story.

Now you've created your own hilarious MAD LIBS® game!

A SPEEDING TICKET

ADJECTIVE _____

VERB ENDING IN "ING" _____

VERB ENDING IN "ING" _____

PLURAL NOUN _____

NOUN _____

NOUN _____

NOUN _____

NOUN _____

ADJECTIVE _____

NOUN _____

PLURAL NOUN _____

PLURAL NOUN _____

NOUN _____

ADVERB _____

NOUN _____

NOUN _____

MAD LIBS®

A SPEEDING TICKET

To be performed by two _____ *people in the room.*
ADJECTIVE

OFFICER: Sir, do you realize how fast you were _____?
VERB ENDING IN "ING"

DRIVER: No, how fast was I _____?
VERB ENDING IN "ING"

OFFICER: You were going fifty _____ per hour in a twenty-five
PLURAL NOUN

_____ zone.
NOUN

DRIVER: I'm sorry. I'm nervous. I'm taking my _____ to the
NOUN

hospital. She's about to have a/an _____.
NOUN

OFFICER: You also went through a red _____ and failed to stop
NOUN

at a/an _____ sign. May I see your driver's _____?
ADJECTIVE   NOUN

DRIVER: Yes. Oh, my! I left it in my other pair of _____. You see,
PLURAL NOUN

my wife started to have labor _____, and I wanted to get her to
PLURAL NOUN

the _____ as _____ as possible.
NOUN   ADVERB

OFFICER: Your wife?

DRIVER: She's right there in the back _____. (*Turns*) Oh, my!
NOUN

Would you believe I forgot my _____, too?
NOUN

MAD LIBS® is fun to play with friends, but you can also play it by yourself! To begin with, DO NOT look at the story on the page below. Fill in the blanks on this page with the words called for. Then, using the words you have selected, fill in the blank spaces in the story.

Now you've created your own hilarious MAD LIBS® game!

SUPERSTITIONS

ADVERB _____

PLURAL NOUN _____

ADJECTIVE _____

PLURAL NOUN _____

PART OF THE BODY _____

ADJECTIVE _____

ANIMAL _____

ADJECTIVE _____

NOUN _____

NUMBER _____

ADJECTIVE _____

VERB _____

PART OF THE BODY _____

ADJECTIVE _____

TYPE OF FOOD _____

PART OF THE BODY _____

MAD◉LIBS®
SUPERSTITIONS

Although we believe ourselves to be _____ civilized, most of

ADVERB

us are really _____ at heart, because we still believe in

PLURAL NOUN

_____ superstitions that began while humans still lived in

ADJECTIVE

_____. Some of these superstitions are:

PLURAL NOUN

1. If you spill salt, throw some over your left _____ for

PART OF THE BODY

_____ luck.

ADJECTIVE

2. If a black _____ runs in front of you, you are in _____

ANIMAL   ADJECTIVE

trouble.

3. If you break a/an _____, you will have _____

NOUN   NUMBER

years of _____ luck.

ADJECTIVE

4. Never _____ under a ladder.

VERB

5. If your _____ itches, it means you will have a/an

PART OF THE BODY

_____ visitor.

ADJECTIVE

6. If you want to keep vampires away from you, always wear _____

TYPE OF FOOD

on a string around your _____.

PART OF THE BODY

MAD LIBS® is fun to play with friends, but you can also play it by yourself! To begin with, DO NOT look at the story on the page below. Fill in the blanks on this page with the words called for. Then, using the words you have selected, fill in the blank spaces in the story.

Now you've created your own hilarious MAD LIBS® game!

FAIRY TALES AND ROMANCE

NOUN _____

NOUN _____

ADJECTIVE _____

PART OF THE BODY (PLURAL) _____

COLOR _____

PLURAL NOUN _____

NOUN _____

VERB ENDING IN "ING" _____

PLURAL NOUN _____

ADJECTIVE _____

ADJECTIVE _____

PLURAL NOUN _____

NOUN _____

ADJECTIVE _____

PART OF THE BODY _____

NOUN _____

NOUN _____

ADVERB _____

MAD LIBS®
FAIRY TALES AND ROMANCE

If a story begins "Once upon a/an _____," you know you are
                                    NOUN

about to read a fairy _____. It is amazing how these _____
                           NOUN   ADJECTIVE

stories remain indelibly etched in our _____. Who can forget
                                        PART OF THE BODY (PLURAL)

Snow _____ *and the Seven* _____, *Beauty and*
            COLOR   PLURAL NOUN

the _____, or *Little Red* _____ *Hood?* Fairy
            NOUN   VERB ENDING IN "ING"

tales introduced us to the magical world of wicked _____; big,
                                                          PLURAL NOUN

_____ wolves; _____ wizards; and dwarfs
      ADJECTIVE   ADJECTIVE

who wore funny _____. These remarkable stories taught us that
                   PLURAL NOUN

good always triumphs over _____ and made us believe in the
                                  NOUN

_____ power of a kiss. Why not? One good smack on the
      ADJECTIVE

_____ could change a frog into a handsome _____,
   PART OF THE BODY   NOUN

enabling him to marry the _____ of his dreams and live, as is
                                  NOUN

written in all these romantic stories, _____ ever after.
                                              ADVERB

MAD LIBS® is fun to play with friends, but you can also play it by yourself! To begin with, DO NOT look at the story on the page below. Fill in the blanks on this page with the words called for. Then, using the words you have selected, fill in the blank spaces in the story.

Now you've created your own hilarious MAD LIBS® game!

SPEAKING OF SPEAKING

ADJECTIVE _____

VERB ENDING IN "ING" _____

PLURAL NOUN _____

NOUN _____

PLURAL NOUN _____

ADJECTIVE _____

PLURAL NOUN _____

PLURAL NOUN _____

NOUN _____

NOUN _____

PART OF THE BODY _____

ADJECTIVE _____

ADJECTIVE _____

PART OF THE BODY _____

TYPE OF LIQUID _____

PART OF THE BODY _____

MAD LIBS®
SPEAKING OF SPEAKING

A recent _____ poll shows that the majority of people are
            ADJECTIVE

terrified of public _____. They would rather walk across
                VERB ENDING IN "ING"

burning _____ or swim in _____-infested
        PLURAL NOUN   NOUN

waters than give a speech in front of a group of _____. This
                                                PLURAL NOUN

_____ fear can be overcome in five easy _____:
    ADJECTIVE   PLURAL NOUN

1. Organize all of your _____ on a piece of _____.
                        PLURAL NOUN   NOUN

2. Remember to start your speech with a funny _____.
                                              NOUN

3. When speaking, look your audience straight in the _____
                                                     PART OF THE BODY

   and speak in a strong and _____ voice.
                             ADJECTIVE

4. Be simple. Never use _____ words that are over the audience's
                        ADJECTIVE

_____.
PART OF THE BODY

5. Always keep a pitcher of _____ next to you, in case your
                            TYPE OF LIQUID

_____ goes dry.
PART OF THE BODY

MAD LIBS® is fun to play with friends, but you can also play it by yourself! To begin with, DO NOT look at the story on the page below. Fill in the blanks on this page with the words called for. Then, using the words you have selected, fill in the blank spaces in the story.

Now you've created your own hilarious MAD LIBS® game!

WHAT NOT TO EAT
FOR LUNCH

ADVERB _____

TYPE OF CONTAINER _____

ADJECTIVE _____

ADJECTIVE _____

SOMETHING ICKY_____

ANIMAL_____

NOUN _____

SILLY WORD _____

PLURAL NOUN_____

VERB ENDING IN "ING"_____

ADJECTIVE _____

SILLY WORD _____

TYPE OF FOOD _____

PLURAL NOUN_____

ANIMAL_____

FOREIGN COUNTRY _____

MAD LIBS®
WHAT NOT TO EAT FOR LUNCH

Everyone knows that kids who eat junk food turn out _____.

ADVERB

Make sure your lunch _____ is filled with nutritious,

TYPE OF CONTAINER

_____ food. Do not go to the _____-food

ADJECTIVE ADJECTIVE

stand across the street from your school. The hamburgers they serve are fried

in _____ and are made of _____ meat. The hot dogs

SOMETHING ICKY ANIMAL

contain chemicals such as hydrogenated _____ and sodium

NOUN

_____. And they are made from ground-up _____.

SILLY WORD PLURAL NOUN

If you spend time _____ around those places, you will get fat

VERB ENDING IN "ING"

and _____, and people will call you a/an _____.

ADJECTIVE SILLY WORD

So take a sandwich made of chicken or turkey, or lettuce, _____,

TYPE OF FOOD

and _____. And drink healthy _____ milk instead

PLURAL NOUN ANIMAL

of cola drinks. If you eat good food, you might grow up to become president of

_____.

FOREIGN COUNTRY

MAD LIBS® is fun to play with friends, but you can also play it by yourself! To begin with, DO NOT look at the story on the page below. Fill in the blanks on this page with the words called for. Then, using the words you have selected, fill in the blank spaces in the story.

Now you've created your own hilarious MAD LIBS® game!

A PAGE FROM A GIRL'S DIARY

ADJECTIVE _____

PERSON IN ROOM (FEMALE) _____

ADJECTIVE _____

NOUN _____

PLURAL NOUN _____

NOUN _____

NOUN _____

NOUN _____

VERB ENDING IN "ING" _____

ADJECTIVE _____

NOUN _____

ADJECTIVE _____

NOUN _____

PERSON IN ROOM (MALE) _____

ADJECTIVE _____

NOUN _____

MAD LIBS®

A PAGE FROM A GIRL'S DIARY

This is a/an _____ entry in _____'s diary.
                 ADJECTIVE   PERSON IN ROOM (FEMALE)

Dear Diary: Today I saw him again. When he looks at me with those

_____ eyes, it makes my _____ go pitter-pat,
      ADJECTIVE   NOUN

and I feel as if I have _____ in my stomach. I think he likes me,
                            PLURAL NOUN

because he asked me for the _____ when I was standing next
                                    NOUN

to him in the _____. I just had to hear his _____
                    NOUN   NOUN

again, so I called his _____ machine and left a/an
                          VERB ENDING IN "ING"

_____ message. I hope he doesn't recognize my _____.
   ADJECTIVE   NOUN

He is such a/an _____ _____, dear Diary. His
                     ADJECTIVE   NOUN

name is _____, and I live with the hope that he will realize how
           PERSON IN ROOM (MALE)

_____ I would be for him, and that I am the _____
   ADJECTIVE   NOUN

he has always been looking for.

MAD LIBS® is fun to play with friends, but you can also play it by yourself! To begin with, DO NOT look at the story on the page below. Fill in the blanks on this page with the words called for. Then, using the words you have selected, fill in the blank spaces in the story.

Now you've created your own hilarious MAD LIBS® game!

THE OSCARS

PLURAL NOUN _____

NOUN _____

NOUN _____

NOUN _____

ADJECTIVE _____

VERB _____

ADJECTIVE _____

PERSON IN ROOM _____

NOUN _____

PART OF THE BODY _____

ADJECTIVE _____

NOUN _____

ADJECTIVE _____

ADJECTIVE _____

ADJECTIVE _____

ADJECTIVE _____

PLURAL NOUN _____

VERB ENDING IN "ING" _____

ADJECTIVE _____

PLURAL NOUN _____

MAD LIBS®
THE OSCARS

Thank you, ladies and _____. I'm so nervous. My _____
                                      PLURAL NOUN   NOUN

is beating a/an _____ a minute. I didn't prepare a/an _____.
                       NOUN   NOUN

I never expected to win this _____ Oscar. I have too many
                                    ADJECTIVE

people to _____. First and foremost, my _____
                    VERB   ADJECTIVE

costar—_____—who was always in my dressing
                         PERSON IN ROOM

_____, held my _____ when I was in trouble,
              NOUN   PART OF THE BODY

and never failed to compliment me or give me a/an _____
                                                   ADJECTIVE

pat on my _____ when I did well. I also want to thank my
                 NOUN

_____ director, my _____ producer, and
      ADJECTIVE   ADJECTIVE

of course, the _____ writer of the screenplay. Most of all, I
                   ADJECTIVE

want to thank you, my _____ fans, and all the members of the
                    ADJECTIVE

Academy of Motion Picture _____ who were responsible
                             PLURAL NOUN

for my _____ this _____ award. Bless your
       VERB ENDING IN "ING"   ADJECTIVE

_____.
     PLURAL NOUN

MAD LIBS® is fun to play with friends, but you can also play it by yourself! To begin with, DO NOT look at the story on the page below. Fill in the blanks on this page with the words called for. Then, using the words you have selected, fill in the blank spaces in the story.

Now you've created your own hilarious MAD LIBS® game!

PENGUIN FACTS

PLURAL NOUN _____

LAST NAME OF PERSON IN ROOM _____

NOUN _____

PLURAL NOUN _____

ADVERB _____

VERB _____

ADJECTIVE _____

PART OF THE BODY (PLURAL) _____

PLURAL NOUN _____

VERB _____

NOUN _____

NOUN _____

PART OF THE BODY (PLURAL) _____

ADJECTIVE _____

PLURAL NOUN _____

PLURAL NOUN _____

MAD LIBS®
PENGUIN FACTS

Fellow bird _____, we are honored to have as our speaker today
　　　　　　　　PLURAL NOUN

Dr. _____, America's foremost _____ on penguins
　　LAST NAME OF PERSON IN ROOM　　　　　　　　　　　　　NOUN

and other cold-climate _____. The doctor has _____ agreed to
　　　　　　　　　　　　PLURAL NOUN　　　　　　　　　ADVERB

answer three questions before we _____ for lunch.
　　　　　　　　　　　　　　　　VERB

DOCTOR: First question, please.

QUESTION: Why do penguins walk in such a/an _____ way?
　　　　　　　　　　　　　　　　　　　　　　ADJECTIVE

DOCTOR: You'd walk funny too if every step you took put your

_____ on frozen _____. Next!
PART OF THE BODY (PLURAL)　　　　　　PLURAL NOUN

QUESTION: How do penguins manage to _____ in such a cold
　　　　　　　　　　　　　　　　　　　VERB

_____?
　　NOUN

DOCTOR: They have an abundance of _____ under their
　　　　　　　　　　　　　　　　　　NOUN

_____. This fat insulates them against _____
PART OF THE BODY (PLURAL)　　　　　　　　　　　　　　ADJECTIVE

weather. Next!

QUESTION: Why do we see only black-and-white penguins?

DOCTOR: Because they're very formal _____. They dress for all
　　　　　　　　　　　　　　　　　PLURAL NOUN

occasions, especially sit-down _____.
　　　　　　　　　　　　　　　PLURAL NOUN

MAD LIBS® is fun to play with friends, but you can also play it by yourself! To begin with, DO NOT look at the story on the page below. Fill in the blanks on this page with the words called for. Then, using the words you have selected, fill in the blank spaces in the story.

Now you've created your own hilarious MAD LIBS® game!

SNOW WHITE

PLURAL NOUN _____

PLURAL NOUN _____

ADJECTIVE _____

NOUN _____

NOUN _____

ADJECTIVE _____

ADJECTIVE _____

NOUN _____

COLOR _____

NOUN _____

PART OF THE BODY _____

NOUN _____

ADVERB _____

MAD LIBS®
SNOW WHITE

One of the most popular fairy _____ of all time is *Snow*
PLURAL NOUN

White and the Seven _____. Snow White is a princess whose
PLURAL NOUN

_____ beauty threatens her stepmother, the queen. Snow
ADJECTIVE

White is forced to flee from the _____ in which she lives and
NOUN

hide in the nearby _____. Once there, she is discovered by
NOUN

_____ animals who guide her to the _____
ADJECTIVE   ADJECTIVE

cottage of the seven dwarfs. The dwarfs take care of her until a prince, who has

traveled the four corners of the _____ in search of Snow
NOUN

_____, arrives and gives her a magical _____
COLOR   NOUN

on her _____, which miraculously brings her back to life after
PART OF THE BODY

she eats a poisonous _____. Snow White and the prince live
NOUN

_____ ever after.
ADVERB

MAD LIBS® is fun to play with friends, but you can also play it by yourself! To begin with, DO NOT look at the story on the page below. Fill in the blanks on this page with the words called for. Then, using the words you have selected, fill in the blank spaces in the story.

Now you've created your own hilarious MAD LIBS® game!

WHAT TO DO WHEN YOU HAVE A COLD

NOUN _____

NOUN _____

PLURAL NOUN _____

NOUN _____

TYPE OF LIQUID _____

NOUN _____

NOUN _____

NOUN _____

NUMBER _____

NOUN _____

EXCLAMATION _____

NOUN _____

ADJECTIVE _____

ADJECTIVE _____

MAD LIBS®
WHAT TO DO WHEN YOU HAVE A COLD

You can always tell when you're getting a cold, because your _____

NOUN

will feel stuffy and you will have a/an _____-ache. The first

NOUN

thing to do is take a couple of _____. Then get into your

PLURAL NOUN

_____ and rest, and drink plenty of _____.

NOUN   TYPE OF LIQUID

Sometimes it's fun being sick. Food is brought to you on a/an _____

NOUN

so you can eat and watch TV, and your temperature is taken by putting a/an

_____ in your _____. If your temperature goes over

NOUN   NOUN

_____ degrees, a doctor should be called. He will thump

NUMBER

you on the _____ and say, "_____!" Then he

NOUN   EXCLAMATION

will ask you what _____ you ate the night before and x-ray your

NOUN

stomach. Finally, he will give you _____ advice on how to get

ADJECTIVE

well. If you do just what he says, you'll feel _____ in no time at all.

ADJECTIVE

MAD LIBS® is fun to play with friends, but you can also play it by yourself! To begin with, DO NOT look at the story on the page below. Fill in the blanks on this page with the words called for. Then, using the words you have selected, fill in the blank spaces in the story.

Now you've created your own hilarious MAD LIBS® game!

PONDERING IN THE POUND

NOUN _____

PART OF THE BODY (PLURAL) _____

ADJECTIVE _____

ADJECTIVE _____

PLURAL NOUN _____

PLURAL NOUN _____

ADJECTIVE _____

ADJECTIVE _____

ADJECTIVE _____

ADJECTIVE _____

ADJECTIVE _____

PLURAL NOUN _____

NOUN _____

PLURAL NOUN _____

ADJECTIVE _____

MAD LIBS®
PONDERING IN THE POUND

I wish I could get out of this crazy _____ and stretch my
                                                NOUN

_____. I sure could use a/an _____ workout. I'll
PART OF THE BODY (PLURAL)   ADJECTIVE

keep my paws crossed that a cute and _____ family will show
                                                  ADJECTIVE

up and take me home. But I have to remember my mom's advice to not base

everything on _____. Just because a family is cute-looking doesn't
                  PLURAL NOUN

mean they're easy to train. Oh, here comes the attendant with two adults and

three little _____. Wow, do they smell _____! This
                PLURAL NOUN   ADJECTIVE

could be the _____ moment. I'd better cool it till I know they're
                  ADJECTIVE

in _____ health and have had their _____ shots.
        ADJECTIVE   ADJECTIVE

Oh, they're picking me up! I hope they don't start making _____
                                                                  ADJECTIVE

faces and silly _____. Hey, they feel cuddly! Forgive me, Mom, but
                  PLURAL NOUN

I'm not going to play it cool. Instead I'm going to give them a welcome wag

with my _____, lick their _____, and throw in
              NOUN   PLURAL NOUN

a/an _____ bark. They won't be able to resist me!
        ADJECTIVE

MAD LIBS® is fun to play with friends, but you can also play it by yourself! To begin with, DO NOT look at the story on the page below. Fill in the blanks on this page with the words called for. Then, using the words you have selected, fill in the blank spaces in the story.

Now you've created your own hilarious MAD LIBS® game!

THE SPACESHIP

VERB ENDING IN "ING" _____

PLURAL NOUN _____

NUMBER _____

NUMBER _____

ADJECTIVE _____

ADJECTIVE _____

NOUN _____

ARTICLE OF CLOTHING (PLURAL) _____

NUMBER _____

TYPE OF METAL _____

ADJECTIVE _____

PLURAL NOUN _____

ADJECTIVE _____

TYPE OF GAS _____

TYPE OF GAS _____

ADVERB _____

VERB _____

MAD LIBS®
THE SPACESHIP

A spaceship is a vehicle used for _____ people between Earth
                                    VERB ENDING IN "ING"

and the distant _____. A journey usually takes _____
                   PLURAL NOUN   NUMBER

years and can cover _____ miles. The passengers have to enter a/an
                        NUMBER

_____ capsule, and will exist in a state of _____
   ADJECTIVE   ADJECTIVE

animation. When the ship reaches its destination, they will hear a/an

_____ and wake up and put on their _____.
   NOUN   ARTICLE OF CLOTHING (PLURAL)

Then they have to land their _____-ton _____ vehicle in a/an
                                NUMBER   TYPE OF METAL

_____ atmosphere. They do this by firing the retro _____.
   ADJECTIVE   PLURAL NOUN

Then they test the atmosphere on this _____ planet to make sure
                                          ADJECTIVE

it contains _____ and is not all _____. If it is okay, then they
              TYPE OF GAS   TYPE OF GAS

can get out of the ship very _____ and _____
                                ADVERB   VERB

all of the inhabitants.

MAD LIBS® is fun to play with friends, but you can also play it by yourself! To begin with, DO NOT look at the story on the page below. Fill in the blanks on this page with the words called for. Then, using the words you have selected, fill in the blank spaces in the story.

Now you've created your own hilarious MAD LIBS® game!

BOBSLEDDING GLOSSARY

PLURAL NOUN _____

ADJECTIVE _____

ADJECTIVE _____

NOUN _____

PLURAL NOUN _____

NOUN _____

NOUN _____

NOUN _____

NOUN _____

PLURAL NOUN _____

PLURAL NOUN _____

NOUN _____

VERB ENDING IN "ING" _____

ADJECTIVE _____

VERB _____

NOUN _____

PLURAL NOUN _____

NOUN _____

MAD LIBS®
BOBSLEDDING GLOSSARY

The name "bobsledding" comes from the early racers bobbing their

_____ back and forth to gain the most _____
　　　PLURAL NOUN　　　　　　　　　　　　　　　　　　　　　　　ADJECTIVE

speed. Here are some _____ phrases to provide a better
　　　　　　　　　　　　　　ADJECTIVE

understanding of this high-speed _____.
　　　　　　　　　　　　　　　　　　NOUN

Bobsled: a large sled made up of two _____ linked together.
　　　　　　　　　　　　　　　　　　　　PLURAL NOUN

There are two sizes, a two-person _____ and a four-_____ sled.
　　　　　　　　　　　　　　　　　NOUN　　　　　　　　　　NOUN

Brakeman: the last _____ to leap onto the _____.
　　　　　　　　　　NOUN　　　　　　　　　　　　　　　　NOUN

He/she applies the _____ to bring it to a stop. The brakeman
　　　　　　　　　　PLURAL NOUN

must have very strong _____.
　　　　　　　　　　　　PLURAL NOUN

Driver: the front _____ in the bobsled, responsible for
　　　　　　　　　　　　　NOUN

_____. The driver's _____ goal is to maintain
VERB ENDING IN "ING"　　　　　　　　　　ADJECTIVE

the straightest path down the track.

Pushtime: the amount of time required to _____ a/an
　　　　　　　　　　　　　　　　　　　　　　　　　VERB

_____ over the first fifty _____ of a run.
　　NOUN　　　　　　　　　　　　　　　　　PLURAL NOUN

WH: abbreviation for "What happened?" Usually said when the _____
　　　　　　　　　　　　　　　　　　　　　　　　　　　　　　　　NOUN

crashes!

MAD LIBS® is fun to play with friends, but you can also play it by yourself! To begin with, DO NOT look at the story on the page below. Fill in the blanks on this page with the words called for. Then, using the words you have selected, fill in the blank spaces in the story.

Now you've created your own hilarious MAD LIBS® game!

WHITE HOUSE TOUR

PLURAL NOUN _____

VERB _____

COLOR _____

ADJECTIVE _____

NOUN _____

NUMBER _____

NOUN _____

ADJECTIVE _____

PLURAL NOUN _____

PLURAL NOUN _____

VERB (PAST TENSE) _____

ROOM _____

CELEBRITY _____

VERB ENDING IN "ING" _____

NOUN _____

NOUN _____

MAD LIBS®
WHITE HOUSE TOUR

Ladies and _____, please _____ this way as
          PLURAL NOUN   VERB

we begin our tour of the _____ House, the _____
                   COLOR   ADJECTIVE

home of our nation's _____. It has more than _____
                  NOUN   NUMBER

rooms! The _____ Room, where huge, _____
           NOUN   ADJECTIVE

_____ are held, is the largest. Throughout the mansion, you will
PLURAL NOUN

find portraits of previous _____ who _____ here.
                  PLURAL NOUN   VERB (PAST TENSE)

Upstairs, you can see the famous Lincoln _____, where the
                                   ROOM

ghost of _____ has often been seen _____.
         CELEBRITY   VERB ENDING IN "ING"

The president's _____ is in the West Wing and is shaped like
                NOUN

a/an _____.
      NOUN

The stories in this book were originally published between 1958 and 2008 by Price Stern Sloan.

MAD LIBS® is fun to play with friends, but you can also play it by yourself! To begin with, DO NOT look at the story on the page below. Fill in the blanks on this page with the words called for. Then, using the words you have selected, fill in the blank spaces in the story.

Now you've created your own hilarious MAD LIBS® game!

FUTURE PROFESSIONS

ADJECTIVE _____

PERSON IN ROOM (FEMALE) _____

VERB ENDING IN "ING" _____

OCCUPATION _____

CELEBRITY (FEMALE) _____

PERSON IN ROOM (MALE) _____

CELEBRITY (MALE) _____

PERSON IN ROOM _____

VERB ENDING IN "ING" _____

PLURAL NOUN_____

NOUN _____

PERSON IN ROOM _____

MAD LIBS®
FUTURE PROFESSIONS

We have all taken an aptitude test and put the results in a/an _____

ADJECTIVE

computer. It predicts that _____ has a lot of talent for

PERSON IN ROOM (FEMALE)

_____. She will probably become a famous _____

VERB ENDING IN "ING" OCCUPATION

like _____. _____ will become a second

CELEBRITY (FEMALE) PERSON IN ROOM (MALE)

_____. On the other hand, _____ should take up

CELEBRITY (MALE) PERSON IN ROOM

_____ and get a job handling _____. When I

VERB ENDING IN "ING" PLURAL NOUN

grow up, I want to be either a fireman, a doctor, or a/an _____.

NOUN

In the meantime, I am modeling myself after my hero, _____.

PERSON IN ROOM

MAD LIBS® is fun to play with friends, but you can also play it by yourself! To begin with, DO NOT look at the story on the page below. Fill in the blanks on this page with the words called for. Then, using the words you have selected, fill in the blank spaces in the story.

Now you've created your own hilarious MAD LIBS® game!

SCUBA DIVING

FIVE LETTERS OF THE ALPHABET_____

NOUN _____

PLURAL NOUN_____

PART OF THE BODY _____

PART OF THE BODY _____

ADJECTIVE _____

VERB _____

NOUN _____

PLURAL NOUN_____

PLURAL NOUN_____

TYPE OF LIQUID_____

PLURAL NOUN_____

NOUN _____

MAD LIBS®
SCUBA DIVING

The word *scuba*, which is spelled _____, means "self-
FIVE LETTERS OF THE ALPHABET

contained underwater breathing _____." A scuba diver wears a tank
NOUN

filled with _____ strapped on his/her _____ and a mask
PLURAL NOUN   PART OF THE BODY

over his/her _____. Divers must be in _____ physical
PART OF THE BODY   ADJECTIVE

condition to _____ under water. Warning! Scuba diving can
VERB

be a very dangerous _____. Divers may run into man-eating
NOUN

_____ or poisonous _____ when they are
PLURAL NOUN   PLURAL NOUN

under-_____. Over the years, scuba divers have discovered many
TYPE OF LIQUID

sunken _____, which have often turned out to be worth a small
PLURAL NOUN

_____.
NOUN

MAD LIBS® is fun to play with friends, but you can also play it by yourself! To begin with, DO NOT look at the story on the page below. Fill in the blanks on this page with the words called for. Then, using the words you have selected, fill in the blank spaces in the story.

Now you've created your own hilarious MAD LIBS® game!

SPOOKY STUFF

ADJECTIVE _____

PLURAL NOUN _____

PLURAL NOUN _____

SILLY WORD _____

TYPE OF LIQUID _____

ADJECTIVE _____

NOUN _____

VERB _____

PLURAL NOUN _____

VERB ENDING IN "ING" _____

NUMBER _____

VERB ENDING IN "ING" _____

PLURAL NOUN _____

NOUN _____

MAD LIBS®
SPOOKY STUFF

American children are fascinated by _____ stuff—like stories
ADJECTIVE

that scare the _____ off them or make their _____
PLURAL NOUN   PLURAL NOUN

stand on end. Scientists say this is because being frightened causes the

_____ gland to function and puts _____ into
SILLY WORD   TYPE OF LIQUID

their blood. And everyone knows that makes kids feel _____.
ADJECTIVE

When they are scared by a movie or a/an _____, boys laugh
NOUN

and holler and _____. But girls cover their eyes with their
VERB

_____ and keep screaming and _____. Most
PLURAL NOUN   VERB ENDING IN "ING"

kids get over this by the time they are _____ years old. Then
NUMBER

they like movies about cars _____ or cops shooting
VERB ENDING IN "ING"

_____, or, if they are girls, they like movies about a boy meeting
PLURAL NOUN

a/an _____ and falling in love. Of course, that can be scary, too.
NOUN

MAD LIBS® is fun to play with friends, but you can also play it by yourself! To begin with, DO NOT look at the story on the page below. Fill in the blanks on this page with the words called for. Then, using the words you have selected, fill in the blank spaces in the story.

Now you've created your own hilarious MAD LIBS® game!

HOW TO HOUSEBREAK A BABY DINOSAUR

NOUN _____

PERSON IN ROOM _____

LETTER OF THE ALPHABET _____

ADJECTIVE _____

VERB (PAST TENSE) _____

NOUN _____

ADJECTIVE _____

ADVERB _____

PLURAL NOUN_____

PLURAL NOUN_____

PART OF THE BODY _____

NOUN _____

PART OF THE BODY _____

PART OF THE BODY (PLURAL) _____

PART OF THE BODY (PLURAL) _____

MAD LIBS®

HOW TO HOUSEBREAK A BABY DINOSAUR

According to the world-famous _____ trainer, _____,
NOUN   PERSON IN ROOM

housebreaking a baby dinosaur is as easy as A, B, _____.
LETTER OF THE ALPHABET

His/Her current _____-selling book, *Down, Dinosaur, Down!*
ADJECTIVE

guarantees that your pet will be potty-_____ in one week or your
VERB (PAST TENSE)

_____ back. This book is filled with _____ advice—
NOUN   ADJECTIVE

it's very _____ written. Here are a few examples:
ADVERB

1. Before you begin training, spread _____ on all the
PLURAL NOUN

   _____ in your house.
   PLURAL NOUN

2. Always call your baby dinosaur by name and look it directly in the

   _____ when giving a command.
   PART OF THE BODY

3. If your baby dinosaur accidentally wets the _____, stay calm
NOUN

   and do not spank its _____.
   PART OF THE BODY

4. All baby dinosaurs respond to praise. When yours performs well, reward it by

   patting its _____ or scratching its _____.
   PART OF THE BODY (PLURAL)   PART OF THE BODY (PLURAL)

MAD LIBS® is fun to play with friends, but you can also play it by yourself! To begin with, DO NOT look at the story on the page below. Fill in the blanks on this page with the words called for. Then, using the words you have selected, fill in the blank spaces in the story.

Now you've created your own hilarious MAD LIBS® game!

NEWSPAPER ADS

ADJECTIVE _____

ADJECTIVE _____

ADJECTIVE _____

ADVERB _____

ADJECTIVE _____

NOUN _____

NOUN _____

ADJECTIVE _____

ADJECTIVE _____

ADJECTIVE _____

NOUN _____

NOUN _____

GEOGRAPHICAL LOCATION _____

ADJECTIVE _____

ADJECTIVE _____

ADJECTIVE _____

PERSON IN ROOM _____

NOUN _____

ADJECTIVE _____

MAD LIBS®
NEWSPAPER ADS

FOR SALE: 1957 Sedan. This _____ car is in a/an _____
ADJECTIVE   ADJECTIVE

condition. It was formerly owned by a/an _____ schoolteacher
ADJECTIVE

who always drove it _____. There is a/an _____
ADVERB   ADJECTIVE

_____ in the backseat and a chrome _____ on the
NOUN   NOUN

hood. It has a/an _____ paint job and _____ tires,
ADJECTIVE   ADJECTIVE

and the back opens out into a/an _____ _____. Will
ADJECTIVE   NOUN

consider taking a slightly used _____ in trade.
NOUN

LOST: In the vicinity of _____, a/an _____
GEOGRAPHICAL LOCATION   ADJECTIVE

French poodle with _____ hair and a/an _____ tail.
ADJECTIVE   ADJECTIVE

It answers to the name of _____ and was last seen carrying a/an
PERSON IN ROOM

_____ in its mouth. A/An _____ reward is offered.
NOUN   ADJECTIVE

MAD LIBS® is fun to play with friends, but you can also play it by yourself! To begin with, DO NOT look at the story on the page below. Fill in the blanks on this page with the words called for. Then, using the words you have selected, fill in the blank spaces in the story.

Now you've created your own hilarious MAD LIBS® game!

HOW TO DO THAT NEW DANCE, THE MONSTROSITY

ADVERB _____

NUMBER _____

PLURAL NOUN_____

VERB _____

PART OF THE BODY (PLURAL) _____

VERB _____

ADVERB _____

PLURAL NOUN_____

PLURAL NOUN_____

PLURAL NOUN_____

SILLY WORD _____

VERB _____

NUMBER _____

VERB _____

MAD LIBS®

HOW TO DO THAT NEW DANCE, THE MONSTROSITY

Two brave volunteers are needed to follow the instructions as they are read.

Here's how you do the Monstrosity: Stand with your feet together. Move your

left foot _____ to the side. Now stamp your right foot _____
           ADVERB   NUMBER

times and put your hands on your partner's _____. Next, you both
                                                     PLURAL NOUN

_____ slowly to the right and bend your _____
     VERB   PART OF THE BODY (PLURAL)

backward. For the next eight counts, both of you _____
                                                     VERB

_____ to the left. Next, you and your partner stand back-to-back
    ADVERB

and wiggle your _____ and slap your _____ together.
              PLURAL NOUN   PLURAL NOUN

Don't forget to keep stamping your right foot. Now, face your partner again,

put your _____ together, and shout, "_____!" Finally,
          PLURAL NOUN   SILLY WORD

_____ backward and repeat the whole thing _____ times.
    VERB   NUMBER

If you feel that you can't learn this dance, you can always _____ the next
                                                           VERB

one out.

MAD LIBS® is fun to play with friends, but you can also play it by yourself! To begin with, DO NOT look at the story on the page below. Fill in the blanks on this page with the words called for. Then, using the words you have selected, fill in the blank spaces in the story.

Now you've created your own hilarious MAD LIBS® game!

HAMLET

CELEBRITY _____

ADJECTIVE _____

NOUN _____

TYPE OF LIQUID_____

NOUN _____

NOUN _____

PLURAL NOUN_____

PLURAL NOUN_____

PLURAL NOUN_____

PLURAL NOUN_____

VERB _____

VERB _____

VERB _____

NOUN _____

MAD LIBS®
HAMLET

This is the soliloquy from the play *Hamlet*, written by _____. In
                                                         CELEBRITY

the third act of this _____ play, Hamlet, who is sometimes called
                            ADJECTIVE

"the melancholy _____," is suspicious of his stepfather and hires
                      NOUN

some actors to act out a scene in which a king is killed, when someone pours

_____ into his _____. First, however, he declaims:
 TYPE OF LIQUID   NOUN

"To be, or not to be: That is the _____: Whether 'tis nobler in the
                                        NOUN

mind to suffer the _____ and _____ of outrageous
                     PLURAL NOUN   PLURAL NOUN

fortune, or to take arms against a sea of _____, and by opposing
                                               PLURAL NOUN

end them? To die: to sleep; no more; and by a sleep to say we end the heartache

and the thousand natural _____ that flesh is heir to, 'tis a
                             PLURAL NOUN

consummation devoutly to be wish'd. To die, to _____; to
                                                        VERB

_____: perchance to _____: ay, there's the _____."
 VERB   VERB   NOUN

MAD LIBS® is fun to play with friends, but you can also play it by yourself! To begin with, DO NOT look at the story on the page below. Fill in the blanks on this page with the words called for. Then, using the words you have selected, fill in the blank spaces in the story.

Now you've created your own hilarious MAD LIBS® game!

A COMMERCIAL MESSAGE FROM THE SPONSOR

ADJECTIVE _____

ADJECTIVE _____

ADJECTIVE _____

NUMBER _____

TYPE OF LIQUID_____

ADJECTIVE _____

TOOTHPASTE BRAND _____

ADJECTIVE _____

ADJECTIVE _____

ADJECTIVE _____

NOUN _____

ADJECTIVE _____

PLURAL NOUN_____

COLOR _____

NOUN _____

MAD LIBS®

A COMMERCIAL MESSAGE FROM THE SPONSOR

Friends, have you noticed that your teeth are beginning to look _____
ADJECTIVE

and _____? That's because you've been using the wrong
ADJECTIVE

toothpaste. Chomp Toothpaste will make your teeth _____ after
ADJECTIVE

only _____ brushings. That's because Chomp Toothpaste contains "hex-a-
NUMBER

chlor-a-_____," a secret ingredient known to your _____
TYPE OF LIQUID   ADJECTIVE

druggist as _____. Chomp attacks the _____ acid in
TOOTHPASTE BRAND   ADJECTIVE

your mouth and leaves your breath _____ and _____.
ADJECTIVE   ADJECTIVE

It will make your _____ feel _____ and will also
NOUN   ADJECTIVE

stimulate your _____. Always keep the familiar _____
PLURAL NOUN   COLOR

tube of Chomp handy in your _____. And now, back to our
NOUN

program.

MAD LIBS® is fun to play with friends, but you can also play it by yourself! To begin with, DO NOT look at the story on the page below. Fill in the blanks on this page with the words called for. Then, using the words you have selected, fill in the blank spaces in the story.

Now you've created your own hilarious MAD LIBS® game!

MY DREAM MAN

ADJECTIVE _____

ADJECTIVE _____

CELEBRITY (MALE) _____

CELEBRITY (MALE) _____

ANIMAL _____

VERB _____

NOUN _____

NOUN _____

PART OF THE BODY _____

ADVERB _____

ADJECTIVE _____

ADVERB _____

ADJECTIVE _____

ADJECTIVE _____

PART OF THE BODY _____

ADJECTIVE _____

NOUN _____

ADJECTIVE _____

PERSON IN ROOM (MALE) _____

MAD LIBS®
MY DREAM MAN

My "dream man" should, first of all, be very _____ and
                                               ADJECTIVE

_____. He should have a physique like _____, a
ADJECTIVE   CELEBRITY (MALE)

profile like _____, and the intelligence of a/an _____.
             CELEBRITY (MALE)   ANIMAL

He must be polite and always remember to _____ my _____,
                                          VERB   NOUN

to tip his _____, and to take my _____ when crossing
           NOUN   PART OF THE BODY

the street. He should move _____, have a/an _____
                           ADVERB   ADJECTIVE

voice, and always dress _____. I would also like him to be a/an
                        ADVERB

_____ dancer, and when we're alone, he should whisper
ADJECTIVE

_____ nothings in my _____ and hold my
ADJECTIVE   PART OF THE BODY

_____ _____. I know a/an _____ man like
ADJECTIVE   NOUN   ADJECTIVE

this is hard to find. In fact, the only one I can think of is _____.
                                                              PERSON IN ROOM (MALE)

MAD LIBS® is fun to play with friends, but you can also play it by yourself! To begin with, DO NOT look at the story on the page below. Fill in the blanks on this page with the words called for. Then, using the words you have selected, fill in the blank spaces in the story.

Now you've created your own hilarious MAD LIBS® game!

ROCK MUSIC

LAST NAME OF PERSON IN ROOM _____

LAST NAME OF PERSON IN ROOM _____

ADJECTIVE _____

PLURAL NOUN _____

PLURAL NOUN _____

ANIMAL (PLURAL) _____

CELEBRITY _____

PLURAL NOUN _____

PLURAL NOUN _____

NOUN _____

NOUN _____

PLURAL NOUN _____

MAD LIBS®
ROCK MUSIC

Young people today would rather listen to a good rock music concert than to

Johann Sebastian _____ or Ludwig van
LAST NAME OF PERSON IN ROOM

_____. Rock music is played by _____
LAST NAME OF PERSON IN ROOM   ADJECTIVE

groups of young men who wear their hair below their _____.
PLURAL NOUN

They also wear very odd and colorful _____ and often have
PLURAL NOUN

beards. The groups have attractive names, such as the _____ or
ANIMAL (PLURAL)

_____ and the Three _____. They usually play
CELEBRITY   PLURAL NOUN

electric _____. One member of the group may sit on a raised
PLURAL NOUN

platform and set the rhythm by beating his _____. The songs they
NOUN

sing are mostly about some fellow who has been rejected by his _____.
NOUN

They are very sad, and when young girls hear them, they often get tears in their

_____.
PLURAL NOUN

MAD LIBS® is fun to play with friends, but you can also play it by yourself! To begin with, DO NOT look at the story on the page below. Fill in the blanks on this page with the words called for. Then, using the words you have selected, fill in the blank spaces in the story.

Now you've created your own hilarious MAD LIBS® game!

LOOKING FOR
BURIED TREASURE

ADJECTIVE _____

PLURAL NOUN _____

ADJECTIVE _____

PLURAL NOUN _____

PLURAL NOUN _____

PLURAL NOUN _____

ADVERB _____

PLURAL NOUN _____

VERB _____

NOUN _____

ADJECTIVE _____

PLURAL NOUN _____

SILLY WORD _____

ADJECTIVE _____

NOUN _____

PLURAL NOUN _____

ADJECTIVE _____

NOUN _____

VERB _____

SAME VERB _____

Are ye looking to get _____ quick? If so, then ye must start searching
                          ADJECTIVE

for buried _____. It's a/an _____ job, but ye might
            PLURAL NOUN   ADJECTIVE

strike it rich and become a multimillionaire. I've heard stories of pirates who

found chests full of gold _____ and sparkling _____,
                           PLURAL NOUN   PLURAL NOUN

and went on to build luxurious _____ and live _____
                                PLURAL NOUN   ADVERB

ever after. But before ye can find buried _____, ye'll need a map
                                            PLURAL NOUN

that shows ye where to _____. Once ye've found the X that marks
                        VERB

the _____, start diggin'. It's best to use a/an _____
     NOUN   ADJECTIVE

shovel, but if ye don't have one, yer bare _____ will do. When ye
                                            PLURAL NOUN

hear _____, ye can stop diggin'. Pull out the chest and look inside.
      SILLY WORD

There might be enough treasure inside to make ye _____. But if
                                                  ADJECTIVE

ye've pulled out a/an _____ filled with sand and _____,
                      NOUN   PLURAL NOUN

don't feel too _____. It's not the end of the _____,
                ADJECTIVE   NOUN

matey. Ye know what they say: If at first ye don't succeed, _____,
                                                             VERB

_____ again.
 SAME VERB

MAD LIBS® is fun to play with friends, but you can also play it by yourself! To begin with, DO NOT look at the story on the page below. Fill in the blanks on this page with the words called for. Then, using the words you have selected, fill in the blank spaces in the story.

Now you've created your own hilarious MAD LIBS® game!

GOING ON A "DIG"

PLURAL NOUN _____

NOUN _____

PLURAL NOUN _____

VERB ENDING IN "ING" _____

ADJECTIVE _____

ONE-SYLLABLE WORD _____

NOUN _____

NUMBER _____

PART OF THE BODY _____

ADJECTIVE _____

TYPE OF FOOD _____

TYPE OF FOOD _____

TYPE OF FOOD _____

NOUN _____

PLURAL NOUN _____

ADJECTIVE _____

ADJECTIVE _____

MAD LIBS®
GOING ON A "DIG"

A "dig" is what archaeologists call it when a bunch of _____ go
PLURAL NOUN

to a desert and look for old bones and pieces of _____ and
NOUN

fossilized _____. _____ and looking for dinosaur
PLURAL NOUN   VERB ENDING IN "ING"

bones is really a/an _____ way to spend a vacation. Last year I dug
ADJECTIVE

up the jawbone of a tyrannosaurus _____. The tyrannosaurus is
ONE-SYLLABLE WORD

my favorite _____. It was _____ feet tall and had a
NOUN   NUMBER

huge _____ with hundreds of _____ teeth. It was
PART OF THE BODY   ADJECTIVE

carnivorous and would eat only _____. The apatosaurus
TYPE OF FOOD

and diplodocus were herbivorous, which means they would eat only

_____, or sometimes _____. If you go on a dig, you
TYPE OF FOOD   TYPE OF FOOD

might also find old pieces of _____, ancient tribal _____,
NOUN   PLURAL NOUN

or pieces of _____ pottery. You can sell these sort of things to
ADJECTIVE

_____ museums and make enough money to pay for your trip.
ADJECTIVE

MAD LIBS® is fun to play with friends, but you can also play it by yourself! To begin with, DO NOT look at the story on the page below. Fill in the blanks on this page with the words called for. Then, using the words you have selected, fill in the blank spaces in the story.

Now you've created your own hilarious MAD LIBS® game!

INTERVIEW WITH A TV HUNK

ADJECTIVE _____

OCCUPATION _____

VERB ENDING IN "ING" _____

ADJECTIVE _____

LETTER OF THE ALPHABET _____

ADJECTIVE _____

VERB _____

PLURAL NOUN _____

ARTICLE OF CLOTHING _____

PLURAL NOUN _____

ADJECTIVE _____

ADJECTIVE _____

MAD LIBS®
INTERVIEW WITH A TV HUNK

INTERVIEWER: Getting right to it, how does it feel to be TV's leading hunk?

HUNK: Strange. I don't really notice it. Offscreen I'm really a/an _____
                                                                   ADJECTIVE

person.

INTERVIEWER: When did you decide you wanted to be a/an _____?
                                                           OCCUPATION

HUNK: I was in a school production of *Hamlet*, and I received a/an

_____ ovation. That did it.
VERB ENDING IN "ING"

INTERVIEWER: Were you a/an _____ student in school?
                                        ADJECTIVE

HUNK: I was a/an _____ student.
                          LETTER OF THE ALPHABET

INTERVIEWER: I understand you are a/an _____ reader. Care to
                                                        ADJECTIVE

_____ your favorites?
VERB

HUNK: Dickens's *A Tale of Two* _____ and Dumas's *The Man in*
                                        PLURAL NOUN

the Iron _____.
        ARTICLE OF CLOTHING

INTERVIEWER: How would you like your _____ to remember you?
                                                  PLURAL NOUN

HUNK: As a/an _____ actor and a/an _____ person.
              ADJECTIVE   ADJECTIVE

MAD LIBS® is fun to play with friends, but you can also play it by yourself! To begin with, DO NOT look at the story on the page below. Fill in the blanks on this page with the words called for. Then, using the words you have selected, fill in the blank spaces in the story.

Now you've created your own hilarious MAD LIBS® game!

MY FAVORITE GURU

ADJECTIVE _____

ADJECTIVE _____

ADJECTIVE _____

ADVERB _____

ADJECTIVE _____

PERSON IN ROOM _____

PLURAL NOUN_____

PLURAL NOUN_____

PLURAL NOUN_____

PERSON IN ROOM _____

NOUN _____

VERB _____

NOUN _____

VERB _____

NOUN _____

MAD LIBS®
MY FAVORITE GURU

If you have _____ problems that keep you from leading a/an
          ADJECTIVE

_____ life, you can generally solve them by _____
   ADJECTIVE   ADJECTIVE

meditation. It has changed my life _____. Every week my friends
                                     ADVERB

and I visit the _____ guru, Mahatma _____. We sit in
         ADJECTIVE   PERSON IN ROOM

a circle with our _____ crossed, we close our _____,
         PLURAL NOUN   PLURAL NOUN

and we make our _____ blank. We begin to chant "Nam yoho
        PLURAL NOUN

_____" over and over. By doing this, we become one with nature
  PERSON IN ROOM

and discover the true _____. If it is impossible for you to visit
               NOUN

a guru, you can _____ alone. All you have to do is find a quiet
         VERB

_____ and meditate and _____ until you achieve
   NOUN   VERB

peace of _____.
     NOUN

MAD LIBS® is fun to play with friends, but you can also play it by yourself! To begin with, DO NOT look at the story on the page below. Fill in the blanks on this page with the words called for. Then, using the words you have selected, fill in the blank spaces in the story.

Now you've created your own hilarious MAD LIBS® game!

HIKING

ADJECTIVE _____

NOUN _____

VERB ENDING IN "ING" _____

ADJECTIVE _____

PLURAL NOUN _____

PART OF THE BODY (PLURAL) _____

DIRECTION _____

ANIMAL (PLURAL) _____

NOUN _____

PLURAL NOUN _____

VERB ENDING IN "ING" _____

ADJECTIVE _____

NUMBER _____

NOUN _____

ADJECTIVE _____

ADVERB _____

MAD LIBS®
HIKING

Hiking is a really _____ thing to do in the summer. But hiking is
_____ADJECTIVE_____

nothing like going for a walk in the _____ or _____
_____NOUN_____VERB ENDING IN "ING"

around the house. The serious hiker needs lots of _____
_____ADJECTIVE

equipment. You must have very comfortable _____ so you won't
_____PLURAL NOUN

make your _____ sore. If you hike in a forest, you must
_____PART OF THE BODY (PLURAL)

take a compass so you can tell which direction is _____, and
_____DIRECTION

you must carry bits of food so you can feed the _____. Every
_____ANIMAL (PLURAL)

good hiker wears a backpack that contains a rolled-up _____
_____NOUN

and some extra _____. If you plan to stay overnight, you must
_____PLURAL NOUN

have a fleece-lined _____ bag. Of course, if you are going up a
_____VERB ENDING IN "ING"

mountain, you will need even more _____ equipment. You will
_____ADJECTIVE

need a/an _____-foot rope and metal pistons to pound into the
_____NUMBER

side of whatever _____ you are scaling. Remember all of these
_____NOUN

_____ tips and you will be able to get back home _____.
ADJECTIVE   ADVERB

MAD LIBS® is fun to play with friends, but you can also play it by yourself! To begin with, DO NOT look at the story on the page below. Fill in the blanks on this page with the words called for. Then, using the words you have selected, fill in the blank spaces in the story.

Now you've created your own hilarious MAD LIBS® game!

A LETTER OF COMPLAINT

NOUN _____

ADJECTIVE _____

NOUN _____

NOUN _____

PLURAL NOUN_____

NOUN _____

PLURAL NOUN_____

VERB ENDING IN "ING" _____

NOUN _____

NOUN _____

ADVERB _____

NOUN _____

PART OF THE BODY (PLURAL) _____

NOUN _____

ADJECTIVE _____

NOUN _____

NOUN _____

NOUN _____

NOUN _____

PLURAL NOUN_____

MAD LIBS®
A LETTER OF COMPLAINT

Dear Sir or _____,
NOUN

I just spent a miserable weekend at your _____ hotel. Your
ADJECTIVE

advertisement in my hometown _____ was an outrageous
NOUN

_____. You said that you provide guests with a welcome basket of
NOUN

_____. All I found in my room was a trash _____
PLURAL NOUN NOUN

filled with old _____. You also claimed to offer free overnight
PLURAL NOUN

_____ in your garage. Not true, fella. Your garage was all filled
VERB ENDING IN "ING"

up, and I had to park my new _____ across the street in a vacant
NOUN

_____. It was stolen! And about your hotel staff—they were
NOUN

_____ inadequate. Your so-called expert masseur not only stuck a
ADVERB

finger in my _____, but he broke two of my _____
NOUN PART OF THE BODY (PLURAL)

while giving me a Swedish _____. Your room service was a/an
NOUN

_____ joke! They not only served burned _____ but spilled
ADJECTIVE NOUN

a hot cup of _____ all over my newly pressed _____. I had
NOUN NOUN

to go to a business meeting wearing a/an _____! I'm planning to
NOUN

sue you for a million _____.
PLURAL NOUN

MAD LIBS® is fun to play with friends, but you can also play it by yourself! To begin with, DO NOT look at the story on the page below. Fill in the blanks on this page with the words called for. Then, using the words you have selected, fill in the blank spaces in the story.

Now you've created your own hilarious MAD LIBS® game!

HAPPY BIRTHDAY!

PERSON IN ROOM (FEMALE) _____

NOUN _____

ADJECTIVE _____

NOUN _____

NUMBER _____

ADJECTIVE _____

PERSON IN ROOM (MALE) _____

NOUN _____

PART OF THE BODY (PLURAL) _____

PLURAL NOUN_____

NOUN _____

ADJECTIVE _____

NOUN _____

NUMBER _____

ADJECTIVE _____

PLURAL NOUN_____

NOUN _____

MAD LIBS®
HAPPY BIRTHDAY!

Friends, this is a surprise party for _____. We are here to
PERSON IN ROOM (FEMALE)

celebrate her _____. All of her most _____
NOUN ADJECTIVE

friends are here, including me, her devoted and faithful _____.
NOUN

I must say that she doesn't look a day over _____. Naturally,
NUMBER

we have some _____ presents for her. _____
ADJECTIVE PERSON IN ROOM (MALE)

brought her a beautiful copper _____ that she can wear on
NOUN

her lovely _____. And our hostess got her a dozen
PART OF THE BODY (PLURAL)

_____ that she can hang in her _____. And we
PLURAL NOUN NOUN

had the bakery send up a huge _____ _____ with
ADJECTIVE NOUN

_____ candles on it. We all want to wish her a very _____
NUMBER ADJECTIVE

birthday and many happy _____. Now, let's all sing together:
PLURAL NOUN

"Happy _____-day to you!"
NOUN

(Editor's note: Sing until all are exhausted.)

MAD LIBS® is fun to play with friends, but you can also play it by yourself! To begin with, DO NOT look at the story on the page below. Fill in the blanks on this page with the words called for. Then, using the words you have selected, fill in the blank spaces in the story.

Now you've created your own hilarious MAD LIBS® game!

WHEN YOU ARE IN LOVE . . .

NOUN _____

NOUN _____

NOUN _____

PLURAL NOUN_____

PART OF THE BODY (PLURAL) _____

NOUN _____

PLURAL NOUN_____

PART OF THE BODY (PLURAL) _____

NOUN _____

VERB _____

PLURAL NOUN_____

NOUN _____

NOUN _____

VERB _____

NOUN _____

PLURAL NOUN_____

PART OF THE BODY _____

MAD LIBS®
WHEN YOU ARE IN LOVE . . .

1. You greet every day with a/an _____ in your heart and a/an
   NOUN

   _____ on your face.
   NOUN

2. You see the whole wide _____ through rose-colored
   NOUN

   _____ and loving _____.
   PLURAL NOUN   PART OF THE BODY (PLURAL)

3. You walk by a babbling _____, spontaneously remove
   NOUN

   your shoes, roll up your _____, sit down, and dangle your
   PLURAL NOUN

   _____ in the sparkling _____.
   PART OF THE BODY (PLURAL)   NOUN

4. You hug and _____ complete _____.
   VERB   PLURAL NOUN

5. You believe beyond the shadow of a/an _____ that you can climb
   NOUN

   the nearest _____ or _____ the deepest _____.
   NOUN   VERB   NOUN

6. You feel good from the tip of your _____ to the top of your
   PLURAL NOUN

   _____.
   PART OF THE BODY

MAD LIBS® is fun to play with friends, but you can also play it by yourself! To begin with, DO NOT look at the story on the page below. Fill in the blanks on this page with the words called for. Then, using the words you have selected, fill in the blank spaces in the story.

Now you've created your own hilarious MAD LIBS® game!

SHOW AND TELL

NOUN _____

VERB ENDING IN "ING" _____

ADVERB _____

SOMETHING ALIVE _____

NOUN _____

ADJECTIVE _____

VERB _____

PERSON IN ROOM _____

ADJECTIVE _____

NOUN _____

TYPE OF FOOD _____

VERB ENDING IN "ING" _____

PLURAL NOUN_____

NOUN _____

NUMBER _____

MAD LIBS®
SHOW AND TELL

Today, I would like to show the class a/an _____ I caught
NOUN

when I went _____ with my aunt. I had never fished before,
VERB ENDING IN "ING"

but my aunt _____ taught me how to bait a hook with a/an
ADVERB

_____ and then how to cast the _____ into
SOMETHING ALIVE   NOUN

the _____ lake. I _____ fishing!
ADJECTIVE   VERB

My name is _____, and I would like to show the class this
PERSON IN ROOM

_____ _____ from my mother's kitchen.
ADJECTIVE   NOUN

My mother uses it every morning to fix my _____. It is
TYPE OF FOOD

also useful if you are into _____ or if you want to slice up
VERB ENDING IN "ING"

some _____. If you want one, you can buy it at your local
PLURAL NOUN

_____ store for only _____ dollars.
NOUN   NUMBER

The stories in this book were originally published between 1958 and 2008 by Price Stern Sloan.

MAD LIBS® is fun to play with friends, but you can also play it by yourself! To begin with, DO NOT look at the story on the page below. Fill in the blanks on this page with the words called for. Then, using the words you have selected, fill in the blank spaces in the story.

Now you've created your own hilarious MAD LIBS® game!

NOTES TO TEACHER

NAME OF TEACHER _____

PERSON IN ROOM (MALE) _____

PART OF THE BODY _____

NOUN _____

ADJECTIVE _____

NUMBER _____

NUMBER _____

NUMBER _____

VERB _____

PLURAL NOUN _____

ADJECTIVE _____

PLURAL NOUN _____

PLURAL NOUN _____

COLOR _____

PLURAL NOUN _____

NOUN _____

MAD LIBS®
NOTES TO TEACHER

Dear _____,
       NAME OF TEACHER

I am writing to ask you to excuse my son, _____,
       PERSON IN ROOM (MALE)

from math class. Trying to do his homework has given him a pain in the

_____. This has caused him to be unable to use a/an
   PART OF THE BODY

_____. He is just like his _____ father, who
   NOUN   ADJECTIVE

adds _____ and _____ and always comes
     NUMBER   NUMBER

up with _____. If you excuse him, he will stay after school and
      NUMBER

_____ the blackboards and dust the _____.
   VERB   PLURAL NOUN

Dear Principal,

Please forgive my daughter for missing her _____ classes yesterday.
               ADJECTIVE

I had to take her to the dentist to get her _____ cleaned and
               PLURAL NOUN

have her _____ measured for braces so that when she is older,
   PLURAL NOUN

she will have straight, _____ _____. If you excuse
         COLOR   PLURAL NOUN

her, I will send you a homemade _____.
              NOUN

MAD LIBS® is fun to play with friends, but you can also play it by yourself! To begin with, DO NOT look at the story on the page below. Fill in the blanks on this page with the words called for. Then, using the words you have selected, fill in the blank spaces in the story.

Now you've created your own hilarious MAD LIBS® game!

ADVERTISEMENT

NOUN _____

NUMBER _____

VERB ENDING IN "ING"_____

VERB ENDING IN "ING"_____

VERB ENDING IN "ING"_____

NOUN _____

ADJECTIVE _____

PLURAL NOUN_____

NOUN _____

ADJECTIVE _____

NOUN _____

ADJECTIVE _____

VERB _____

PERSON IN ROOM _____

NOUN _____

NOUN _____

NOUN _____

NOUN _____

SILLY WORD _____

NOUN _____

MAD LIBS®
ADVERTISEMENT

Seeking a new career? Be a/an _____—or just look like one! In just
NOUN

_____ sessions, we can have you _____,
NUMBER   VERB ENDING IN "ING"

_____, and _____ like a top-playing
VERB ENDING IN "ING"   VERB ENDING IN "ING"

_____. Opportunities in this _____ field
NOUN   ADJECTIVE

are limitless. There is no fee! Just come in for a free consultation. Our expert

_____ will analyze your _____ and determine
PLURAL NOUN   NOUN

your potential for success in this _____ field. Use your natural
ADJECTIVE

_____ to earn _____ money and have time
NOUN   ADJECTIVE

to _____ your dreams, too. Just ask _____, who
VERB   PERSON IN ROOM

came to us looking like a/an _____ out of _____,
NOUN   NOUN

and in just ten days improved his/her _____ 100 percent. We
NOUN

even corrected his/her horrible _____. It was just in the nick
NOUN

of time, because the _____ Squad was ready to ban him/her
SILLY WORD

from the _____. Don't wait another day. Time is running out.
NOUN

MAD LIBS® is fun to play with friends, but you can also play it by yourself! To begin with, DO NOT look at the story on the page below. Fill in the blanks on this page with the words called for. Then, using the words you have selected, fill in the blank spaces in the story.

Now you've created your own hilarious MAD LIBS® game!

POOL RULES

NOUN _____

ADJECTIVE _____

ADJECTIVE _____

VERB ENDING IN "ING" _____

ADJECTIVE _____

PLURAL NOUN _____

ADJECTIVE _____

PLURAL NOUN _____

NUMBER _____

NOUN _____

NOUN _____

VERB ENDING IN "ING" _____

ADJECTIVE _____

NOUN _____

ADJECTIVE _____

PLURAL NOUN _____

ADVERB _____

PART OF THE BODY _____

ADJECTIVE _____

NOUN _____

ADJECTIVE _____

MAD LIBS
POOL RULES

ATTENTION ALL SWIMMERS!

If you want to swim in this _____ or soak in our _____
                              NOUN   ADJECTIVE

spa, you must follow these _____ rules.
                                ADJECTIVE

1. No _____ allowed. Men must wear _____
         VERB ENDING IN "ING"   ADJECTIVE

    shorts, and women must wear one-piece bathing _____
                                                         PLURAL NOUN

    or _____ bikinis.
            ADJECTIVE

2. No _____ under the age of _____ are allowed
         PLURAL NOUN   NUMBER

    in the _____ unless accompanied by a/an _____.
              NOUN   NOUN

3. _____ in the pool is only permitted in the _____
     VERB ENDING IN "ING"   ADJECTIVE

    end, and only when a life-_____ is on duty.
                                  NOUN

4. People with _____ hair must wear bathing _____.
                    ADJECTIVE   PLURAL NOUN

WARNING! If you plan to sunbathe, _____ cover your arms,
                                         ADVERB

legs, and _____ with a/an _____ lotion. You
              PART OF THE BODY   ADJECTIVE

don't want to get a/an _____-burn!
                            NOUN

Have a/an _____ day!
                ADJECTIVE

MAD LIBS® is fun to play with friends, but you can also play it by yourself! To begin with, DO NOT look at the story on the page below. Fill in the blanks on this page with the words called for. Then, using the words you have selected, fill in the blank spaces in the story.

Now you've created your own hilarious MAD LIBS® game!

A RECIPE FOR ICE CUBES

ADJECTIVE _____

NOUN _____

NOUN _____

VERB _____

TYPE OF LIQUID_____

TYPE OF LIQUID_____

TYPE OF LIQUID_____

COLOR _____

VERB _____

VERB _____

NUMBER _____

ADJECTIVE _____

ADVERB _____

PART OF THE BODY (PLURAL) _____

VERB _____

VERB _____

MAD LIBS®

A RECIPE FOR ICE CUBES

To make _____ ice cubes, first find a tray with a mold shaped
             ADJECTIVE

like a/an _____ or a/an _____. Then
         NOUN   NOUN

_____ once while holding the tray. Fill the molds with
     VERB

_____ or even _____ (but for the best
  TYPE OF LIQUID   TYPE OF LIQUID

results, always use _____). It can even be dyed _____ if
           TYPE OF LIQUID   COLOR

you wish. _____ carefully when placing the tray in the freezer.
       VERB

Allow the cubes to _____ for at least _____
           VERB   NUMBER

minutes, or until they are completely _____. Remove the tray
                      ADJECTIVE

_____, and jiggle with your _____ until the
   ADVERB   PART OF THE BODY (PLURAL)

cubes _____. Add to your favorite drink and _____.
   VERB   VERB

MAD LIBS® is fun to play with friends, but you can also play it by yourself! To begin with, DO NOT look at the story on the page below. Fill in the blanks on this page with the words called for. Then, using the words you have selected, fill in the blank spaces in the story.

Now you've created your own hilarious MAD LIBS® game!

WAITER AND CUSTOMER

NOUN _____

NOUN _____

TYPE OF FOOD _____

NOUN _____

ADJECTIVE _____

NOUN _____

ADJECTIVE _____

ADJECTIVE _____

NOUN _____

NOUN _____

ADJECTIVE _____

NOUN _____

ADJECTIVE _____

TYPE OF LIQUID _____

MAD LIBS®

WAITER AND CUSTOMER

SCENE: A restaurant—where else?

CUSTOMER: Oh, waiter! Would you please bring me a/an _____? I
                                                          NOUN

want to see what today's specials are.

WAITER: Today's specials are cream of _____ soup and T-bone
                                              NOUN

_____. Does that sound good?
    TYPE OF FOOD

CUSTOMER: Yes, but I'll have the roast prime _____ of beef
                                                      NOUN

with the _____ pudding.
            ADJECTIVE

WAITER: We're out of that. How about a sizzling sirloin _____
                                                              NOUN

and a/an _____ green salad?
            ADJECTIVE

CUSTOMER: No, thanks, I'd rather have the _____ fried chicken.
                                                ADJECTIVE

WAITER: Sorry, but we're out of that, too. How about soft-shell _____?
                                                                      NOUN

CUSTOMER: No, thanks. Do you have any roast Long Island _____?
                                                              NOUN

WAITER: Sorry, no. Why don't you try our _____ goulash with
                                                ADJECTIVE

homemade _____ sauce?
                NOUN

CUSTOMER: No, thanks. Just bring me a/an _____ egg sandwich
                                                ADJECTIVE

and a cup of black _____.
                      TYPE OF LIQUID

MAD LIBS® is fun to play with friends, but you can also play it by yourself! To begin with, DO NOT look at the story on the page below. Fill in the blanks on this page with the words called for. Then, using the words you have selected, fill in the blank spaces in the story.

Now you've created your own hilarious MAD LIBS® game!

MAGIC, ANYONE?

PLURAL NOUN _____

ADJECTIVE _____

ADJECTIVE _____

NOUN _____

NOUN _____

NOUN _____

NOUN _____

ADJECTIVE _____

PART OF THE BODY _____

PLURAL NOUN _____

ADJECTIVE _____

NOUN _____

ADJECTIVE _____

NOUN _____

PART OF THE BODY (PLURAL) _____

PART OF THE BODY _____

PLURAL NOUN _____

MAD LIBS®
MAGIC, ANYONE?

_____ of all ages enjoy watching _____
  PLURAL NOUN   ADJECTIVE

magicians perform their _____ tricks. Every man, woman, and
                                    ADJECTIVE

_____ loves to see a magician pull a/an _____ out
        NOUN   NOUN

of a hat, saw a live _____ in half, or make a huge _____
                              NOUN   NOUN

disappear into _____ air. Audiences love when magicians perform
                          ADJECTIVE

sleight of _____ with a deck of _____,
                  PART OF THE BODY   PLURAL NOUN

a/an _____ coin, or a silk _____. The greatest of
              ADJECTIVE   NOUN

all magicians was the _____ Harry Houdini, who was able to
                                ADJECTIVE

escape from a locked _____ even though his _____
                                NOUN   PART OF THE BODY (PLURAL)

were tied behind his _____ and his feet were wrapped in iron
                                PART OF THE BODY

_____.
        PLURAL NOUN

MAD LIBS® is fun to play with friends, but you can also play it by yourself! To begin with, DO NOT look at the story on the page below. Fill in the blanks on this page with the words called for. Then, using the words you have selected, fill in the blank spaces in the story.

Now you've created your own hilarious MAD LIBS® game!

COMMERCIAL FOR FACE CREAM

PLURAL NOUN _____

NOUN _____

ADJECTIVE _____

NOUN _____

NOUN _____

ADJECTIVE _____

CELEBRITY _____

ADJECTIVE _____

PLURAL NOUN _____

ADJECTIVE _____

NOUN _____

NUMBER _____

NOUN _____

MAD LIBS®
COMMERCIAL FOR FACE CREAM

And now, ladies and _____, an important commercial message
                        PLURAL NOUN

from our _____, the manufacturer of new, improved ALL-GOO,
              NOUN

the face cream for women. ALL-GOO now contains a new _____
                                                          ADJECTIVE

ingredient called "hexa-mone," which is made from distilled _____
                                                                  NOUN

juice. If you put ALL-GOO on your _____ every evening,
                                        NOUN

your complexion will look as _____ as a daisy. The famous
                                  ADJECTIVE

Hollywood star _____ says, "I use ALL-GOO every day, and my
                    CELEBRITY

complexion is always _____ and my _____
                          ADJECTIVE   PLURAL NOUN

always have a youthful glow." Yes, ALL-GOO is the _____ cream of
                                                      ADJECTIVE

the stars. Remember, if you want a softer, smoother _____, get
                                                          NOUN

ALL-GOO in the handy _____-pound size at your friendly
                          NUMBER

neighborhood _____ store.
                  NOUN

MAD LIBS® is fun to play with friends, but you can also play it by yourself! To begin with, DO NOT look at the story on the page below. Fill in the blanks on this page with the words called for. Then, using the words you have selected, fill in the blank spaces in the story.

Now you've created your own hilarious MAD LIBS® game!

THE FAMILY THAT PLAYS TOGETHER . . .

PLURAL NOUN _____

ADJECTIVE _____

NOUN _____

NOUN _____

ADJECTIVE _____

NOUN _____

NOUN _____

PART OF THE BODY _____

PLURAL NOUN _____

VERB _____

NOUN _____

NOUN _____

ADJECTIVE _____

NOUN _____

NOUN _____

ADJECTIVE _____

ADJECTIVE _____

NOUN _____

MAD LIBS®
THE FAMILY THAT PLAYS TOGETHER . . .

Some of my fondest _____ from my _____ childhood
                         PLURAL NOUN   ADJECTIVE

are of my father teaching my siblings and me to play _____-
                                               NOUN

ball, foot-_____, and other _____ sports. He
                NOUN   ADJECTIVE

never said we'd end up in the Super _____ or the World
                                     NOUN

_____, but he did teach us to put our _____
      NOUN   PART OF THE BODY

and soul into the game and play to the best of our _____. "It
                                        PLURAL NOUN

isn't whether you win or _____," he would say, "but how you
                              VERB

play the _____." He bought us a volley-_____
           NOUN   NOUN

and put up a/an _____ net in our back-_____,
                ADJECTIVE   NOUN

and he also taught us how to play tennis on the public courts near our

_____. We were so lucky to have a/an _____
      NOUN   ADJECTIVE

family that did so many _____ things together. Like they always
                          ADJECTIVE

say, the _____ that plays together, stays together!
           NOUN

MAD LIBS® is fun to play with friends, but you can also play it by yourself! To begin with, DO NOT look at the story on the page below. Fill in the blanks on this page with the words called for. Then, using the words you have selected, fill in the blank spaces in the story.

Now you've created your own hilarious MAD LIBS® game!

NEWSPAPER STORY

CITY _____

VERB ENDING IN "ING" _____

ADJECTIVE _____

CITY _____

NAME OF PERSON (MALE) _____

VEHICLE _____

PLURAL NOUN _____

COLOR _____

NOUN _____

SOMETHING ALIVE (PLURAL) _____

PLURAL NOUN _____

COLOR _____

SILLY WORD _____

ADJECTIVE _____

SAME CITY _____

ADJECTIVE _____

MAD LIBS®
NEWSPAPER STORY

Last Thursday, two _____ men were _____
CITY   VERB ENDING IN "ING"

in a/an _____ field near _____, Indiana.
ADJECTIVE   CITY

Suddenly, one of them said, "Hey, _____, look up there at that
NAME OF PERSON (MALE)

bright, silvery _____ floating over our _____!" And
VEHICLE   PLURAL NOUN

before his friend could reply, a powerful _____ light shot down
COLOR

and lifted them into a strange flying _____. Inside, they were
NOUN

greeted by tiny green _____ and given a dinner of French-
SOMETHING ALIVE (PLURAL)

fried _____ and _____ beans. Afterward, they flew to
PLURAL NOUN   COLOR

planet _____ and met its _____ inhabitants. Then the flying
SILLY WORD   ADJECTIVE

machine brought them back to _____, Indiana. The men told our
SAME CITY

reporter that it was a really _____ experience.
ADJECTIVE

MAD LIBS® is fun to play with friends, but you can also play it by yourself! To begin with, DO NOT look at the story on the page below. Fill in the blanks on this page with the words called for. Then, using the words you have selected, fill in the blank spaces in the story.

Now you've created your own hilarious MAD LIBS® game!

THE THREE BRANCHES OF GOVERNMENT

PLURAL NOUN _____

NOUN _____

PLURAL NOUN _____

ADJECTIVE _____

PLURAL NOUN _____

OCCUPATION _____

VERB ENDING IN "S" _____

VERB ENDING IN "ING" _____

NOUN _____

VERB (PAST TENSE) _____

NOUN _____

ADJECTIVE _____

PLURAL NOUN _____

PLURAL NOUN _____

PLURAL NOUN _____

SAME OCCUPATION _____

MAD LIBS®
THE THREE BRANCHES OF GOVERNMENT

Our founding _____ designed our _____
               PLURAL NOUN   NOUN

with three main branches. This was to protect the _____
                                                        PLURAL NOUN

from a/an _____ leader. The three branches form a system of
              ADJECTIVE

checks and _____.
                PLURAL NOUN

THE EXECUTIVE BRANCH includes the office of _____. This
                                                 OCCUPATION

branch _____ the judicial and legislative branches and has
           VERB ENDING IN "S"

_____ power.
   VERB ENDING IN "ING"

THE JUDICIAL BRANCH is responsible for upholding the _____,
                                                          NOUN

which was _____ by our founding fathers. The judicial branch
              VERB (PAST TENSE)

includes a Supreme _____, which rules on _____ issues.
                       NOUN   ADJECTIVE

THE LEGISLATIVE BRANCH is divided into two _____—the
                                               PLURAL NOUN

House of Representatives and the Senate. Together they regulate which

_____ are passed into _____. This branch,
    PLURAL NOUN   PLURAL NOUN

however, can be vetoed by the _____.
                                 SAME OCCUPATION

MAD LIBS® is fun to play with friends, but you can also play it by yourself! To begin with, DO NOT look at the story on the page below. Fill in the blanks on this page with the words called for. Then, using the words you have selected, fill in the blank spaces in the story.

Now you've created your own hilarious MAD LIBS® game!

ANSWERS TO ANIMAL QUESTIONS

PLURAL NOUN _____

TYPE OF LIQUID _____

TYPE OF MATERIAL _____

NOUN _____

GREETING _____

EXCLAMATION _____

NOUN _____

PLURAL NOUN _____

NUMBER _____

ADJECTIVE _____

PART OF THE BODY _____

PART OF THE BODY _____

TYPE OF LIQUID _____

ADJECTIVE _____

MAD LIBS®
ANSWERS TO ANIMAL QUESTIONS

QUESTION: Why do camels have _____?
                                        PLURAL NOUN

ANSWER: Camels live in the desert and have to go for days without food or

_____. Their humps are made of _____, on
        TYPE OF LIQUID   TYPE OF MATERIAL

which they live.

QUESTION: Can dogs talk?

ANSWER: A dog is talking when he wags his _____ or when
                                                        NOUN

he barks. If a dog wags his tail, it can mean "_____" or
                                                          GREETING

"_____!"
        EXCLAMATION

QUESTION: When frightened, does an ostrich stick its _____ in the sand?
                                                                  NOUN

ANSWER: No, it can run away very fast because it has such long _____.
                                                                    PLURAL NOUN

QUESTION: What is the biggest land animal alive today?

ANSWER: The elephant. It weighs _____ tons. It has a/an
                                              NUMBER

_____ trunk, which it uses like we use our _____
        ADJECTIVE   PART OF THE BODY

or our _____. When it is hot, an elephant squirts
                PART OF THE BODY

_____ on its back with its _____ trunk.
        TYPE OF LIQUID   ADJECTIVE

MAD LIBS® is fun to play with friends, but you can also play it by yourself! To begin with, DO NOT look at the story on the page below. Fill in the blanks on this page with the words called for. Then, using the words you have selected, fill in the blank spaces in the story.

Now you've created your own hilarious MAD LIBS® game!

GOLF

SILLY WORD _____

NOUN _____

NOUN _____

ADJECTIVE _____

NOUN _____

NOUN _____

PLURAL NOUN _____

NOUN _____

TYPE OF LIQUID _____

PLURAL NOUN _____

NOUN _____

NOUN _____

ADVERB _____

PART OF THE BODY _____

NOUN _____

EXCLAMATION _____

NOUN _____

MAD LIBS®
GOLF

The word *golf* comes from the German word _____ which
SILLY WORD

means *club*. Golf is an outdoor _____ played on a large
NOUN

_____ with a small, _____ ball. You use a
NOUN   ADJECTIVE

club with a long, slender _____ and a metal or wooden
NOUN

_____ to hit the ball into a series of eighteen _____.
NOUN   PLURAL NOUN

When you play golf, you try to keep the ball in the middle of the _____
NOUN

and try to avoid _____ hazards and sand _____.
TYPE OF LIQUID   PLURAL NOUN

Before you attempt to play golf, you should take lessons from a professional

_____ who will teach you how to swing a _____
NOUN   NOUN

and putt _____. Important: To avoid hitting another player in
ADVERB

the _____ or on top of the _____, be sure
PART OF THE BODY   NOUN

to yell, "_____!" This warns them that a/an _____
EXCLAMATION   NOUN

is headed their way.

The stories in this book were originally published between 1958 and 2008 by Price Stern Sloan.
Copyright © Penguin Random House LLC.

MAD LIBS® is fun to play with friends, but you can also play it by yourself! To begin with, DO NOT look at the story on the page below. Fill in the blanks on this page with the words called for. Then, using the words you have selected, fill in the blank spaces in the story.

Now you've created your own hilarious MAD LIBS® game!

CAVEMEN

ADJECTIVE _____

PLURAL NOUN _____

NOUN _____

ADJECTIVE _____

PLURAL NOUN _____

PART OF THE BODY (PLURAL) _____

PLURAL NOUN _____

PLURAL NOUN _____

SILLY WORD _____

SILLY WORD _____

NOUN _____

ADJECTIVE _____

ADJECTIVE _____

ADJECTIVE _____

ADJECTIVE _____

NOUN _____

ADJECTIVE _____

NOUN _____

MAD LIBS®
CAVEMEN

Some scientists think of cavemen as the _____ link between
ADJECTIVE

modern man and _____. Cavemen were intelligent, especially the
PLURAL NOUN

Neanderthals, who created the bow and _____, which enabled
NOUN

them to hunt _____ animals. They used the skins of these
ADJECTIVE

_____ to cover their _____ and also to keep
PLURAL NOUN   PART OF THE BODY (PLURAL)

their _____ warm. They learned to make fire by rubbing two
PLURAL NOUN

_____ together. Although at first they could only make sounds
PLURAL NOUN

such as "_____" and "_____," which roughly
SILLY WORD   SILLY WORD

translate to "Hello" and "Where's the _____'s room?" Eventually,
NOUN

they developed their own _____ language. If a Neanderthal man
ADJECTIVE

were around today, with his _____ brain, _____
ADJECTIVE   ADJECTIVE

muscles, and _____ face, he would make a great president of a/an
ADJECTIVE

_____ company, or at the very least, a/an _____
NOUN   ADJECTIVE

used-_____ salesman.
NOUN

MAD LIBS® is fun to play with friends, but you can also play it by yourself! To begin with, DO NOT look at the story on the page below. Fill in the blanks on this page with the words called for. Then, using the words you have selected, fill in the blank spaces in the story.

Now you've created your own hilarious MAD LIBS® game!

HOW TO GO TO SLEEP

ADJECTIVE _____

ADJECTIVE _____

TYPE OF LIQUID _____

ADJECTIVE _____

ADJECTIVE _____

ADVERB _____

ADJECTIVE _____

PLURAL NOUN _____

ADJECTIVE _____

ADJECTIVE _____

PLURAL NOUN _____

NOUN _____

PLURAL NOUN _____

NOUN _____

ADJECTIVE _____

ADJECTIVE _____

PART OF THE BODY _____

MAD LIBS®
HOW TO GO TO SLEEP

If you have trouble falling asleep, you probably have a/an _____
                                                        ADJECTIVE

mind. You must learn to relax so you will have a/an _____
                                                    ADJECTIVE

mind instead. First, drink a cup of hot _____ and stretch out
                                        TYPE OF LIQUID

on a/an _____ bed in a/an _____ position.
        ADJECTIVE   ADJECTIVE

Then, breathe _____ and think about something beautiful, such
              ADVERB

as _____ _____. Do not think about your _____
   ADJECTIVE   PLURAL NOUN   ADJECTIVE

enemies or entertain any other _____ thoughts. Concentrate on
                               ADJECTIVE

something restful, such as _____, which will make your
                           PLURAL NOUN

_____ more relaxed, or count imaginary _____
NOUN   PLURAL NOUN

jumping over a/an _____. Follow these _____
                  NOUN   ADJECTIVE

rules and you will fall into a/an _____ sleep the minute your
                                  ADJECTIVE

_____ hits the pillow.
PART OF THE BODY

MAD LIBS® is fun to play with friends, but you can also play it by yourself! To begin with, DO NOT look at the story on the page below. Fill in the blanks on this page with the words called for. Then, using the words you have selected, fill in the blank spaces in the story.

Now you've created your own hilarious MAD LIBS® game!

SAMSON AND DELILAH
(A TRAGIC DIALOGUE)

ADJECTIVE _____

PLURAL NOUN _____

NOUN _____

ADJECTIVE _____

NOUN _____

ANIMAL _____

EXCLAMATION _____

ADJECTIVE _____

VERB _____

NOUN _____

ADJECTIVE _____

NOUN _____

ADJECTIVE _____

MAD LIBS®

SAMSON AND DELILAH (A TRAGIC DIALOGUE)

DELILAH: Sam Samson! Will you stop doing those _____ exercises?
    ADJECTIVE

SAMSON: Listen, Delilah. I have to keep my _____ in shape. After
    PLURAL NOUN

all, I'm the strongest _____ in the tribe.
    NOUN

DELILAH: Well, you look _____. Look at the way your hair hangs
    ADJECTIVE

down over your _____.
    NOUN

SAMSON: I've been busy. Yesterday I had to kill ten thousand Philistines with

the jawbone of a/an _____.
    ANIMAL

DELILAH: _____! You promised to take me to a/an
    EXCLAMATION

_____ party tonight.
    ADJECTIVE

SAMSON: Okay. So I'll _____ my hair.
    VERB

DELILAH: I'll do it for you. Now just sit here on this _____ and
    NOUN

I'll give you a/an _____ haircut.
    ADJECTIVE

SAMSON: Okay.

DELILAH: There. Your _____ is nice and short. How do you feel?
    NOUN

SAMSON: _____.
    ADJECTIVE

MAD LIBS® is fun to play with friends, but you can also play it by yourself! To begin with, DO NOT look at the story on the page below. Fill in the blanks on this page with the words called for. Then, using the words you have selected, fill in the blank spaces in the story.

Now you've created your own hilarious MAD LIBS® game!

E-MAIL ETIQUETTE

VERB ENDING IN "ING" _____

CITY _____

LANGUAGE _____

ADJECTIVE _____

ADJECTIVE _____

VERB ENDING IN "ING" _____

PLURAL NOUN _____

VERB ENDING IN "ING" _____

VERB _____

ADJECTIVE _____

VERB _____

VERB ENDING IN "ING" _____

ADJECTIVE _____

PLURAL NOUN _____

PLURAL NOUN _____

ADVERB _____

TYPE OF FOOD (PLURAL) _____

ADJECTIVE _____

MAD LIBS®
E-MAIL ETIQUETTE

When _____ to your relatives in _____ or to
        VERB ENDING IN "ING"   CITY

your _____ teacher, it's _____ to make your
           LANGUAGE   ADJECTIVE

e-mails as simple and _____ as possible. Here are some tips for
                           ADJECTIVE

_____ the perfect e-mail:
VERB ENDING IN "ING"

• Make sure that you don't write in all capital _____—it will
                                                    PLURAL NOUN

sound like you're _____.
                  VERB ENDING IN "ING"

• It's important to _____ your words correctly. Otherwise,
                          VERB

people will think you are _____ and that you don't take enough
                              ADJECTIVE

time to _____ your e-mails before you send them.
             VERB

• Write to someone as if you're actually _____ to them. It's very
                                         VERB ENDING IN "ING"

_____ to write in incomplete _____ and use the
    ADJECTIVE   PLURAL NOUN

wrong _____.
       PLURAL NOUN

• Try to get to the point of your e-mail as _____ as possible.
                                                ADVERB

Since many people don't even have the time anymore to sit down and eat

_____ with their families, be as _____ with your
TYPE OF FOOD (PLURAL)   ADJECTIVE

e-mails as possible.

MAD LIBS® is fun to play with friends, but you can also play it by yourself! To begin with, DO NOT look at the story on the page below. Fill in the blanks on this page with the words called for. Then, using the words you have selected, fill in the blank spaces in the story.

Now you've created your own hilarious MAD LIBS® game!

FIREFIGHTERS

ADJECTIVE _____

ADJECTIVE _____

NOUN _____

NOUN _____

PLURAL NOUN _____

NUMBER _____

PLURAL NOUN _____

NOUN _____

NOUN _____

ADJECTIVE _____

TYPE OF LIQUID _____

PLURAL NOUN _____

ADJECTIVE _____

NOUN _____

PLURAL NOUN _____

NOUN _____

MAD LIBS
FIREFIGHTERS

When I was ten years old, my _____ ambition in life was to be a
ADJECTIVE

firefighter—but here I am, nothing but a/an _____ _____.
ADJECTIVE   NOUN

If I were a firefighter, I'd get to wear a huge red _____. And I could
NOUN

ride on the fire engines that carry eighty-foot _____ and travel
PLURAL NOUN

_____ miles per hour. When fire engines blow their _____, all
NUMBER   PLURAL NOUN

cars have to pull over to the side of the _____. Fire departments
NOUN

have hook-and-_____ wagons as well as pump trucks, which
NOUN

carry _____ hoses that pump _____ into burning
ADJECTIVE   TYPE OF LIQUID

_____. Firefighters have to go into _____ buildings
PLURAL NOUN   ADJECTIVE

and fight their way through smoke and _____ to rescue any
NOUN

_____ who may be trapped inside. We should all be thankful that
PLURAL NOUN

our firefighters are on the job twenty-four hours a/an _____.
NOUN

MAD LIBS® is fun to play with friends, but you can also play it by yourself! To begin with, DO NOT look at the story on the page below. Fill in the blanks on this page with the words called for. Then, using the words you have selected, fill in the blank spaces in the story.

Now you've created your own hilarious MAD LIBS® game!

MORE THAN YOU NEED TO KNOW ABOUT PIRATES

ADJECTIVE _____

PLURAL NOUN _____

PLURAL NOUN _____

ADJECTIVE _____

PLURAL NOUN _____

NUMBER _____

PLURAL NOUN _____

ADJECTIVE _____

VERB _____

NOUN _____

PLURAL NOUN _____

PLURAL NOUN _____

PLURAL NOUN _____

PLURAL NOUN _____

ADJECTIVE _____

ADVERB _____

PLURAL NOUN _____

PART OF THE BODY (PLURAL) _____

NOUN _____

MAD LIBS®

MORE THAN YOU NEED TO KNOW ABOUT PIRATES

Pirates were known by many different _____ names. They were
                                        ADJECTIVE

called buccaneers, freebooters, corsairs, and _____. A high
                                               PLURAL NOUN

percentage of pirates wore beards and _____ to cover the
                                        PLURAL NOUN

_____ scars on their faces. The average buccaneer was five
    ADJECTIVE

feet, seven _____ tall and weighed _____
               PLURAL NOUN   NUMBER

_____. Most freebooters were without any _____
    PLURAL NOUN   ADJECTIVE

education. They could not _____ or even write their own _____.
                            VERB   NOUN

Although pirates are portrayed in classic novels and motion _____
                                                             PLURAL NOUN

as romantic _____, in truth, they were feisty _____
               PLURAL NOUN   PLURAL NOUN

with short _____ and _____ tempers. They
              PLURAL NOUN   ADJECTIVE

_____ believed that actions speak louder than _____
   ADVERB   PLURAL NOUN

and, armed to the _____, would fight at the drop of a/an
                   PART OF THE BODY (PLURAL)

_____.
    NOUN

MAD LIBS® is fun to play with friends, but you can also play it by yourself! To begin with, DO NOT look at the story on the page below. Fill in the blanks on this page with the words called for. Then, using the words you have selected, fill in the blank spaces in the story.

Now you've created your own hilarious MAD LIBS® game!

ARMY INFORMATION

ADJECTIVE _____

ADJECTIVE _____

PLURAL NOUN _____

PLURAL NOUN _____

NOUN _____

NOUN _____

ADVERB _____

ADJECTIVE _____

PLURAL NOUN _____

NOUN _____

PLURAL NOUN _____

ADJECTIVE _____

EXCLAMATION _____

NOUN _____

NOUN _____

ADJECTIVE _____

NOUN _____

MAD LIBS®
ARMY INFORMATION

If you plan on joining the army, here are some _____ hints that
                                                    ADJECTIVE

will help you become a/an _____ soldier. The army is made up
                                 ADJECTIVE

of officers, non-coms, and _____. You can recognize officers by
                                  PLURAL NOUN

the _____ on their shoulders and the _____
         PLURAL NOUN   NOUN

on their caps. When you address an officer, always say "_____"
                                                                    NOUN

and salute _____. If you get a/an _____ haircut,
                 ADVERB   ADJECTIVE

keep your _____ shined, and see that your _____
               PLURAL NOUN   NOUN

is clean at all times, you will be a credit to the slogan, "The army builds

_____." And at roll call, when the _____ sergeant
      PLURAL NOUN   ADJECTIVE

calls your name, shout "_____!" loud and clear. Also, become
                              EXCLAMATION

familiar with basic weapons such as the thirty-caliber _____ and the
                                                              NOUN

automatic _____. Follow this advice and in no time you'll win the
               NOUN

_____ Conduct _____.
      ADJECTIVE   NOUN

MAD LIBS® is fun to play with friends, but you can also play it by yourself! To begin with, DO NOT look at the story on the page below. Fill in the blanks on this page with the words called for. Then, using the words you have selected, fill in the blank spaces in the story.

Now you've created your own hilarious MAD LIBS® game!

MEDICAL QUESTIONS AND ANSWERS

PERSON IN ROOM _____

PERSON IN ROOM _____

ADJECTIVE _____

NOUN _____

NOUN _____

NOUN _____

NOUN _____

ADJECTIVE _____

ADJECTIVE _____

ADJECTIVE _____

NOUN _____

TYPE OF LIQUID_____

PLURAL NOUN_____

NUMBER _____

PART OF THE BODY _____

NOUN _____

NOUN _____

MAD LIBS®
MEDICAL QUESTIONS AND ANSWERS

The patient is to be played by _____, *and the doctor is to be*
PERSON IN ROOM

played by _____.
PERSON IN ROOM

PATIENT: Doctor, whenever I stand up I get a/an _____ pain in
ADJECTIVE

my _____. Is this serious?
NOUN

DOCTOR: Sounds as if you have an inflammation of your _____.
NOUN

You need an anti-_____ shot.
NOUN

PATIENT: Doctor, I'm thinking of having my _____ removed. Is
NOUN

this a/an _____ operation?
ADJECTIVE

DOCTOR: No, the operation is quite _____, provided that you
ADJECTIVE

have _____ kidneys.
ADJECTIVE

PATIENT: What are the symptoms of an overactive _____?
NOUN

DOCTOR: High _____ pressure. Also, severe _____
TYPE OF LIQUID   PLURAL NOUN

in the abdomen.

PATIENT: Doctor, is it possible for a/an _____-year-old man to
NUMBER

have a/an _____ attack?
PART OF THE BODY

DOCTOR: Only if he doesn't watch his _____ and eats too much _____.
NOUN   NOUN

MAD LIBS® is fun to play with friends, but you can also play it by yourself! To begin with, DO NOT look at the story on the page below. Fill in the blanks on this page with the words called for. Then, using the words you have selected, fill in the blank spaces in the story.

Now you've created your own hilarious MAD LIBS® game!

ROMEO AND JULIET

NOUN _____

PLURAL NOUN _____

NOUN _____

ADJECTIVE _____

PLURAL NOUN _____

ADVERB _____

PLURAL NOUN _____

PLURAL NOUN _____

PLURAL NOUN _____

LANGUAGE _____

VERB (PAST TENSE) _____

PLURAL NOUN _____

PLURAL NOUN _____

ADJECTIVE _____

NOUN _____

NOUN _____

LAST NAME OF PERSON IN ROOM _____

MAD LIBS®
ROMEO AND JULIET

If you believe William Shakespeare's *Romeo and Juliet* to be the greatest

_____ story ever written, you will not find many _____
       NOUN   PLURAL NOUN

who disagree. This tragic _____ of two _____
                                NOUN   ADJECTIVE

teenagers who come from rival _____ and fall _____
                             PLURAL NOUN   ADVERB

in love has captivated _____ for more than four hundred
                        PLURAL NOUN

_____. It has been translated into more than a hundred different
   PLURAL NOUN

_____, including _____. Even those who have
     PLURAL NOUN   LANGUAGE

not read or _____ the play know the story of these star-crossed
              VERB (PAST TENSE)

_____. Many can quote _____ from the _____
   PLURAL NOUN   PLURAL NOUN   ADJECTIVE

soliloquy that Romeo delivers when he climbs a/an _____ to get
                                          NOUN

onto Juliet's _____. Scholars agree that *Romeo and Juliet* ranks
               NOUN

up there with *Hamlet*, *Othello*, and *King* _____.
                                            LAST NAME OF PERSON IN ROOM

MAD LIBS® is fun to play with friends, but you can also play it by yourself! To begin with, DO NOT look at the story on the page below. Fill in the blanks on this page with the words called for. Then, using the words you have selected, fill in the blank spaces in the story.

Now you've created your own hilarious MAD LIBS® game!

THE PROM

PART OF THE BODY _____

PART OF THE BODY _____

ADJECTIVE _____

NOUN _____

NOUN _____

ADJECTIVE _____

PLURAL NOUN _____

NOUN _____

NOUN _____

PLURAL NOUN _____

ADJECTIVE _____

VERB ENDING IN "ING" _____

ADJECTIVE _____

NOUN _____

NOUN _____

NOUN _____

MAD LIBS®
THE PROM

If there's a melody you can't seem to get out of your _____ or
PART OF THE BODY

a song running through your _____, then bring your feet to this
PART OF THE BODY

year's _____ prom. As usual, our _____ will be
ADJECTIVE   NOUN

held in our high school _____. A dress code will be observed. No
NOUN

one will be admitted wearing _____ or torn _____.
ADJECTIVE   PLURAL NOUN

Girls must wear a/an _____, and boys must wear a dress shirt
NOUN

and a/an _____. As always, hot _____ will be
NOUN   PLURAL NOUN

served, and there will be _____ prizes and an award for the best-
ADJECTIVE

_____ couple. The _____ dance committee
VERB ENDING IN "ING"   ADJECTIVE

is also proud to announce that every girl who attends will receive a/an

_____ to pin to her _____, and every boy will
NOUN   NOUN

receive a complimentary _____.
NOUN

MAD LIBS® is fun to play with friends, but you can also play it by yourself! To begin with, DO NOT look at the story on the page below. Fill in the blanks on this page with the words called for. Then, using the words you have selected, fill in the blank spaces in the story.

Now you've created your own hilarious MAD LIBS® game!

MY FAVORITE TEACHER CONTEST

ADJECTIVE _____

CELEBRITY (FEMALE) _____

ADJECTIVE _____

SCHOOL _____

PLURAL NOUN _____

ADJECTIVE _____

ADJECTIVE _____

PART OF THE BODY _____

CELEBRITY (MALE) _____

ADJECTIVE _____

VERB _____

ADVERB _____

VERB _____

CELEBRITY _____

LETTER OF THE ALPHABET _____

ROOM _____

PLURAL NOUN _____

PIECE OF FURNITURE (PLURAL) _____

NOUN _____

MAD LIBS®
MY FAVORITE TEACHER CONTEST

Dear School Board,

I heard you were running a contest to pick the most _____
                                                        ADJECTIVE

teacher in town. I would like to nominate _____, who teaches
                                            CELEBRITY (FEMALE)

history and _____ studies at _____. She is always
                  ADJECTIVE   SCHOOL

patient with her _____, no matter how _____
                     PLURAL NOUN   ADJECTIVE

or _____ we get. Yesterday she asked, "Who is president of
        ADJECTIVE

the United States?" and I held up my _____ and said,
                                          PART OF THE BODY

"_____." My answer was incorrect, but she didn't
      CELEBRITY (MALE)

get _____ or _____ _____ or
        ADJECTIVE   VERB   ADVERB

even make me _____ in the corner. She gave me a second
                    VERB

chance and asked, "Who is buried in Grant's Tomb?" I knew that one. I answered,

"_____." And for a grade, she gave me a/an _____.
      CELEBRITY   LETTER OF THE ALPHABET

She also doesn't mind when we have to go to the _____, and doesn't
                                                       ROOM

get mad if we throw _____ or hide under the _____.
                         PLURAL NOUN   PIECE OF FURNITURE (PLURAL)

I hope you pick her as the world's best _____.
                                             NOUN

MAD LIBS® is fun to play with friends, but you can also play it by yourself! To begin with, DO NOT look at the story on the page below. Fill in the blanks on this page with the words called for. Then, using the words you have selected, fill in the blank spaces in the story.

Now you've created your own hilarious MAD LIBS® game!

HOROSCOPE

NOUN _____

ADJECTIVE _____

PLURAL NOUN_____

ADJECTIVE _____

SILLY WORD _____

NOUN _____

PLURAL NOUN_____

PLURAL NOUN_____

ADJECTIVE _____

PLURAL NOUN_____

ADJECTIVE _____

ADJECTIVE _____

ADJECTIVE _____

PLURAL NOUN_____

ADJECTIVE _____

ADJECTIVE _____

PLURAL NOUN_____

ADJECTIVE _____

ADJECTIVE _____

MAD LIBS®
HOROSCOPE

Those born under the planetary sign of the _____ possess a/an
NOUN

_____ personality and are forever searching for new _____
ADJECTIVE   PLURAL NOUN

to conquer. This is a more or less _____ month for you, because the
ADJECTIVE

planet _____ is directly over your _____
SILLY WORD   NOUN

and Mercury is influencing your _____.This means you should
PLURAL NOUN

avoid eating _____ and stay away from anybody with
PLURAL NOUN

_____ _____. During the coming year,
ADJECTIVE   PLURAL NOUN

you will find conditions getting _____ due to your
ADJECTIVE

_____ outlook on life and your _____
ADJECTIVE   ADJECTIVE

attitude toward _____.You are best suited to a/an _____
PLURAL NOUN   ADJECTIVE

mate with _____ _____ and a/an
ADJECTIVE   PLURAL NOUN

_____ complexion, which means, of course, that you can
ADJECTIVE

look forward to a really _____ life.
ADJECTIVE

MAD LIBS® is fun to play with friends, but you can also play it by yourself! To begin with, DO NOT look at the story on the page below. Fill in the blanks on this page with the words called for. Then, using the words you have selected, fill in the blank spaces in the story.

Now you've created your own hilarious MAD LIBS® game!

LOOK IT UP

ADJECTIVE _____

NOUN _____

NOUN _____

PLURAL NOUN _____

ADVERB _____

ADVERB _____

NOUN _____

NOUN _____

NOUN _____

NOUN _____

PLURAL NOUN _____

PLURAL NOUN _____

ADVERB _____

NOUN _____

NOUN _____

NOUN _____

NOUN _____

NOUN _____

NOUN _____

MAD LIBS®
LOOK IT UP

A/An _____ dictionary is the essential reference _____
     ADJECTIVE   NOUN

for home, school, or _____. A dictionary not only defines
                          NOUN

_____ but tells you how to spell words _____
  PLURAL NOUN   ADVERB

and how to pronounce them _____. Dictionaries are available
                                ADVERB

in local _____-stores, or, if necessary, you can order one with a/an
            NOUN

_____ card over the Internet. For the average _____, a
     NOUN   NOUN

medium-sized dictionary is best. For researchers, an unabridged _____,
                                                                    NOUN

which has more than two hundred thousand _____, will be useful.
                                              PLURAL NOUN

For those who can't remember the meaning of any _____,
                                                    PLURAL NOUN

a pocket-sized dictionary works _____. These dictionaries are
                                    ADVERB

small enough to fit in a woman's _____, the pocket of a
                                      NOUN

man's _____, or in a kid's back-_____. As Henry
         NOUN   NOUN

Wadsworth Longfellow, the famous _____, wrote, "I'd rather go
                                      NOUN

without food in my _____ than go without a dictionary on my
                        NOUN

_____-shelf."
     NOUN

MAD LIBS® is fun to play with friends, but you can also play it by yourself! To begin with, DO NOT look at the story on the page below. Fill in the blanks on this page with the words called for. Then, using the words you have selected, fill in the blank spaces in the story.

Now you've created your own hilarious MAD LIBS® game!

GOOD MANNERS

NOUN _____

NOUN _____

NOUN _____

VERB _____

PART OF THE BODY _____

ADVERB _____

NOUN _____

NOUN _____

NOUN _____

NOUN _____

PART OF THE BODY (PLURAL) _____

NOUN _____

ADJECTIVE _____

ADVERB _____

MAD LIBS®
GOOD MANNERS

1. When you receive a birthday _____ or a wedding
   NOUN

   _____, you should always send a thank-you _____.
   NOUN   NOUN

2. When you _____ or burp out loud, be sure to cover your
   VERB

   _____ and say, "I'm _____ sorry."
   PART OF THE BODY   ADVERB

3. If you are a man and wearing a/an _____ on your head and a/an
   NOUN

   _____ approaches, it's always polite to tip your _____.
   NOUN   NOUN

4. When you are at a friend's _____ for dinner, remember, it's not
   NOUN

   polite to eat with your _____, take food from anyone else's
   PART OF THE BODY (PLURAL)

   _____, or leave the table before everyone else.
   NOUN

5. When meeting your friend's parents, always try to make a/an _____
   ADJECTIVE

   impression by greeting them _____.
   ADVERB

MAD LIBS® is fun to play with friends, but you can also play it by yourself! To begin with, DO NOT look at the story on the page below. Fill in the blanks on this page with the words called for. Then, using the words you have selected, fill in the blank spaces in the story.

Now you've created your own hilarious MAD LIBS® game!

MY DREAM GIRL

ADJECTIVE _____

COLOR _____

PLURAL NOUN _____

ADJECTIVE _____

TYPE OF LIQUID _____

ADJECTIVE _____

PLURAL NOUN _____

ADJECTIVE _____

NOUN _____

PERSON IN ROOM _____

EXCLAMATION _____

ADJECTIVE _____

ADJECTIVE _____

ADJECTIVE _____

ADJECTIVE _____

NOUN _____

PLURAL NOUN _____

ADJECTIVE _____

PERSON IN ROOM (FEMALE) _____

MAD LIBS®
MY DREAM GIRL

The girl of my dreams has _____ _____ hair
ADJECTIVE   COLOR

scented like _____. Her eyes are like two _____
PLURAL NOUN   ADJECTIVE

pools of _____. And her lips remind me of _____
TYPE OF LIQUID   ADJECTIVE

_____. Her skin is as smooth and lovely as a/an _____
PLURAL NOUN   ADJECTIVE

_____, and she has a figure like _____. When
NOUN   PERSON IN ROOM

she enters a room, people always stare at her and say, "_____! What
EXCLAMATION

a/an _____ woman!" Her sense of humor is always _____, and
ADJECTIVE   ADJECTIVE

people marvel at her _____ vocabulary. In my dreams I see her
ADJECTIVE

wearing a/an _____ dress and a diamond _____
ADJECTIVE   NOUN

in her hair. I would gladly give up all my _____ for one evening
PLURAL NOUN

with this _____ girl. Her name is _____.
ADJECTIVE   PERSON IN ROOM (FEMALE)

MAD LIBS® is fun to play with friends, but you can also play it by yourself! To begin with, DO NOT look at the story on the page below. Fill in the blanks on this page with the words called for. Then, using the words you have selected, fill in the blank spaces in the story.

Now you've created your own hilarious MAD LIBS® game!

MARK ANTONY'S ADDRESS FROM *JULIUS CAESAR*

PLURAL NOUN _____

PLURAL NOUN _____

VERB _____

PLURAL NOUN _____

NAME OF PERSON _____

ADJECTIVE _____

PLURAL NOUN _____

NOUN _____

NOUN _____

NOUN _____

NOUN _____

NOUN _____

PLURAL NOUN _____

NOUN _____

MAD LIBS®

MARK ANTONY'S ADDRESS FROM *JULIUS CAESAR*

Friends, Romans, _____, lend me your _____; I
                        PLURAL NOUN   PLURAL NOUN

come to _____ Caesar, not to praise him. The evil that men do
                     VERB

lives after them; the good is oft interred with their _____; so let
                                             PLURAL NOUN

it be with _____. The noble Brutus hath told you Caesar was
                 NAME OF PERSON

_____: if it were so, it was a grievous fault. If you have _____,
ADJECTIVE   PLURAL NOUN

prepare to shed them now. You all do know this _____. I
                                              NOUN

remember the first time ever Caesar put it on. Through this the well-beloved

Brutus stabb'd; for Brutus, as you know, was Caesar's _____: This
                                                   NOUN

was the most unkindest _____ of all. Here is the _____,
                         NOUN   NOUN

and under Caesar's seal. To every Roman _____ he gives,
                                             NOUN

to every several man, seventy-five _____. Here was a/an
                                      PLURAL NOUN

_____! When comes such another?
NOUN

MAD LIBS® is fun to play with friends, but you can also play it by yourself! To begin with, DO NOT look at the story on the page below. Fill in the blanks on this page with the words called for. Then, using the words you have selected, fill in the blank spaces in the story.

Now you've created your own hilarious MAD LIBS® game!

TO WHOM IT MAY CONCERN

PERSON IN ROOM _____

NUMBER _____

ADVERB _____

NOUN _____

ADJECTIVE _____

VERB _____

ADJECTIVE _____

PLURAL NOUN _____

SAME PERSON IN ROOM _____

NOUN _____

PLURAL NOUN _____

NUMBER _____

SAME PERSON IN ROOM _____

ADJECTIVE _____

NOUN _____

VERB _____

MAD LIBS®
TO WHOM IT MAY CONCERN

I have known _____ for _____ years
 PERSON IN ROOM   NUMBER

and _____ recommend him/her for the position of assistant
          ADVERB

_____ in your _____ company. I can't _____
      NOUN   ADJECTIVE   VERB

enough about this person's _____ character and ability to get
                                   ADJECTIVE

along with his/her fellow _____. As for educational background,
                               PLURAL NOUN

_____ is a college _____ and is capable of speaking
 SAME PERSON IN ROOM   NOUN

several foreign _____, and has an IQ of _____. You will
                   PLURAL NOUN   NUMBER

find _____ to be a/an _____ worker who is not
      SAME PERSON IN ROOM   ADJECTIVE

only as smart as a/an _____, but who doesn't know the meaning
                            NOUN

of the word _____. Unfortunately, this is one of many words this
                   VERB

person doesn't know the meaning of.

MAD LIBS® is fun to play with friends, but you can also play it by yourself! To begin with, DO NOT look at the story on the page below. Fill in the blanks on this page with the words called for. Then, using the words you have selected, fill in the blank spaces in the story.

Now you've created your own hilarious MAD LIBS® game!

SCENE BETWEEN A PARENT AND A TEACHER

PERSON IN ROOM _____

PERSON IN ROOM _____

SCHOOL_____

PERSON IN ROOM (MALE) _____

NOUN _____

PLURAL NOUN_____

NOUN _____

NOUN _____

ADJECTIVE _____

PLURAL NOUN_____

PERSON IN ROOM (FEMALE) _____

ARTICLE OF CLOTHING _____

ADVERB _____

NOUN _____

ADJECTIVE _____

SCENE BETWEEN A PARENT AND A TEACHER

To be read by _____ *and* _____.
      PERSON IN ROOM   PERSON IN ROOM

TEACHER: I asked you to come to _____ because I am so worried
                                      SCHOOL

about your son, _____.
                PERSON IN ROOM (MALE)

PARENT: Oh, I am sure he has been a very good _____. We have
                                                      NOUN

always taught him to mind his _____.
                                  PLURAL NOUN

TEACHER: Well, yesterday I caught him copying from someone else's

_____.
      NOUN

PARENT: I cannot believe that our little _____ would do anything
                                              NOUN

that _____.
        ADJECTIVE

TEACHER: And on Monday, he stole three _____ from
                                              PLURAL NOUN

_____'s _____.
PERSON IN ROOM (FEMALE)   ARTICLE OF CLOTHING

PARENT: Well, he always behaves very _____ at home.
                                          ADVERB

TEACHER: I hope you will talk to your _____ about these problems.
                                          NOUN

PARENT: I will, I will. I'll ground him and take away his _____
                                                              ADJECTIVE

privileges.

MAD LIBS® is fun to play with friends, but you can also play it by yourself! To begin with, DO NOT look at the story on the page below. Fill in the blanks on this page with the words called for. Then, using the words you have selected, fill in the blank spaces in the story.

Now you've created your own hilarious MAD LIBS® game!

LOVE LETTER

ADJECTIVE _____

NOUN _____

NOUN _____

ADJECTIVE _____

ADJECTIVE _____

NOUN _____

NOUN _____

NOUN _____

PART OF THE BODY _____

NOUN _____

NOUN _____

ADJECTIVE _____

PLURAL NOUN _____

PART OF THE BODY _____

PART OF THE BODY _____

NOUN _____

VERB _____

NOUN _____

PART OF THE BODY _____

VERB _____

PERSON IN ROOM _____

MAD LIBS®
LOVE LETTER

My _____ darling,
_{ADJECTIVE}

I love you more than _____ itself. Each minute away from
_{NOUN}

you is a/an _____, each hour a/an _____
_{NOUN} _{ADJECTIVE}

eternity. Without you, life is empty, boring, and _____. I
_{ADJECTIVE}

feel like a baby without my _____, a toddler without my teddy
_{NOUN}

_____, a dog without its _____. I can't get you out
_{NOUN} _{NOUN}

of my _____. I can't stop thinking about the color of your
_{PART OF THE BODY}

_____, the way you wear your _____, your
_{NOUN} _{NOUN}

_____ laugh. This morning, when the mailman brought your
_{ADJECTIVE}

special delivery _____, my _____ skipped a beat,
_{PLURAL NOUN} _{PART OF THE BODY}

my _____ was in my throat, and my _____
_{PART OF THE BODY} _{NOUN}

trembled so much, I could hardly _____. What you said set my
_{VERB}

_____ on fire. Do write again. Until then, I love you from the
_{NOUN}

bottom of my _____.
_{PART OF THE BODY}

I will _____ you always, _____
_{VERB} _{PERSON IN ROOM}

MAD LIBS® is fun to play with friends, but you can also play it by yourself! To begin with, DO NOT look at the story on the page below. Fill in the blanks on this page with the words called for. Then, using the words you have selected, fill in the blank spaces in the story.

Now you've created your own hilarious MAD LIBS® game!

WHY DO SKUNKS SMELL?

NOUN _____

ADJECTIVE _____

PLURAL NOUN_____

A PLACE_____

PLURAL NOUN_____

ADJECTIVE _____

NOUN _____

VERB ENDING IN "ING" _____

PART OF THE BODY _____

PART OF THE BODY (PLURAL) _____

PART OF THE BODY (PLURAL) _____

ADVERB _____

COLOR _____

PART OF THE BODY _____

PART OF THE BODY _____

MAD LIBS®
WHY DO SKUNKS SMELL?

Surprisingly, a skunk is a friendly _____ who can make a/an
                                          NOUN

_____ household pet. But what makes these _____
        ADJECTIVE   PLURAL NOUN

smell to high (the) _____? The skunk has scent _____
                         A PLACE   PLURAL NOUN

that contain a/an _____-smelling fluid. When attacked, the skunk
                        ADJECTIVE

aims this smelly _____ at its enemies. But the skunk does give
                        NOUN

warning before _____. It raises its _____ or
                   VERB ENDING IN "ING"   PART OF THE BODY

stamps its _____ so that you can run away as fast as your
              PART OF THE BODY (PLURAL)

_____ can carry you. The most _____
   PART OF THE BODY (PLURAL)   ADVERB

recognizable skunk is the one with a/an _____ line on its
                                              COLOR

_____ and another one between its _____ and
   PART OF THE BODY   PART OF THE BODY

its ears.

MAD LIBS® is fun to play with friends, but you can also play it by yourself! To begin with, DO NOT look at the story on the page below. Fill in the blanks on this page with the words called for. Then, using the words you have selected, fill in the blank spaces in the story.

Now you've created your own hilarious MAD LIBS® game!

A (SECRET) LETTER FROM AN ADMIRER

PERSON IN ROOM (FEMALE) _____

NOUN _____

ADJECTIVE _____

ADJECTIVE _____

PERSON IN ROOM _____

ADJECTIVE _____

ADJECTIVE _____

PLURAL NOUN _____

ADJECTIVE _____

ADJECTIVE _____

ADJECTIVE _____

ADJECTIVE _____

ADJECTIVE _____

ADJECTIVE _____

ADJECTIVE _____

ADJECTIVE _____

ADJECTIVE _____

NOUN _____

ADVERB _____

PERSON IN ROOM (MALE) _____

MAD LIBS®
A (SECRET) LETTER FROM AN ADMIRER

Dear Miss _____,
_____PERSON IN ROOM (FEMALE)

You may not recall my _____, but I met you at the _____
NOUN ADJECTIVE

cocktail party given by our _____ friend, _____.
ADJECTIVE PERSON IN ROOM

We had a/an _____ talk about _____
ADJECTIVE ADJECTIVE

_____, and I was impressed by your _____
PLURAL NOUN ADJECTIVE

conversation and your grasp of the _____ situation. Also, I was
ADJECTIVE

very much attracted to your _____ eyes, your _____
ADJECTIVE ADJECTIVE

little chin, and your _____ teeth. If you'll pardon me for seeming
ADJECTIVE

_____, I was fascinated by your _____ walk and
ADJECTIVE ADJECTIVE

by your _____ figure. I hope I made a/an _____
ADJECTIVE ADJECTIVE

impression and that we can get together for a nice _____ next
NOUN

week.

_____ yours,
ADVERB

_____
PERSON IN ROOM (MALE)

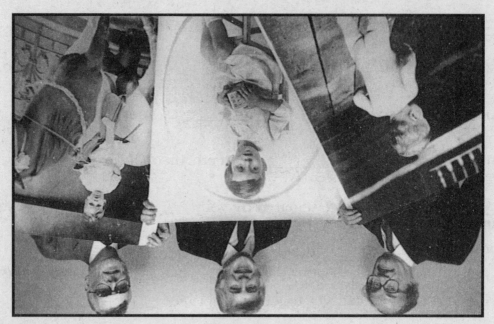

Roger Price, Leonard Stern, and Larry Sloan

MAD LIBS®
LEONARD STERN

Leonard Stern has created, written, directed, and produced an unprecedented twenty-three television series. He has won Emmy Awards for *The Honeymooners*, *The Phil Silvers Show (Sgt. Bilko)*, and *Get Smart*. He was honored with the Peabody Award for *The Steve Allen Show*. The Academy of Television Arts & Sciences and the Writers Guild of America have nominated him for numerous awards. Mr. Stern's theatrical movie writing credits include such films as *Abbott and Costello in the Foreign Legion*, *The Jazz Singer*, and *Three for the Money*.

Leonard Stern was president of the Producers Guild of America, which awarded him with the Charles Fitzsimons Honorary Lifetime Member Award. He was chairman of the Caucus for Television Producers, Writers & Directors, receiving the Distinguished Service Award and Member of the Year Award. Mr. Stern also served as chairman of the American Film Institute's Feature Film and Television Development Program.

Leonard Stern collaborated with Roger Price to create *Mad Libs*, and along with Mr. Price and Larry Sloan, he formed publisher Price Stern Sloan.

MAD LIBS®
ROGER PRICE

Roger Price, cofounder of Price Stern Sloan, was a highly acclaimed comedy writer. He started his career writing for Bob Hope on the radio, and in the 1940s and 1950s continued to work with Hope in both radio and newspaper outlets. Mr. Price was instrumental in starting a radio program called *The Comedy Writer's Show*. He also performed in nightclubs and on Broadway, receiving the prestigious Donaldson Award as the most promising newcomer. In the 1950s, he developed his classic *Droodles* cartoons.

By the late 1950s, Roger Price had joined forces with Leonard Stern, and together they created *Mad Libs*, the classic party game that Steve Allen used as a warm-up for guests on his TV show. *Mad Libs* served as the launch title for a fledgling publishing company which, when joined by Larry Sloan, became Price Stern Sloan—then the largest trade book publisher on the West Coast.

Roger Price continued to write and publish such popular books as *The World's Worst Elephant Jokes* in 1963 and *The World's Worst Jokes* in 1969. In the 1980s, Mr. Price acted in numerous television shows and movies. His humor and warm personality live on through the smiles and laughter he brought to people all over the world through *Mad Libs*.

MAD LIBS®
L.L. (LARRY) SLOAN

L.L. (Larry) Sloan joined Roger Price and Leonard Stern in 1962 to create Price Stern Sloan, which became the largest trade publisher on the West Coast. Mr. Sloan was executive editor and CEO until the company was sold in 1993.

Born in Manhattan, Mr. Sloan attended New York City public schools, including DeWitt Clinton High School, where he and Mr. Stern became friends writing for the student newspaper and the senior musical comedy. Mr. Sloan attended UCLA and Stanford and served in the Army and Air Force in World War II. His first postwar job was at the *Hollywood Citizen-News*, where he began as a reporter covering movie studios and became a film and drama critic with a daily column. During this period, he was a Hollywood correspondent for the *London Evening News* and was part of a weekly ABC radio show called *Hollywood Byline*. He also wrote for various national magazines.

In the early 1950s, Mr. Sloan became a public relations and advertising consultant, working on large campaigns including the opening of Disneyland and the Sahara Hotel in Las Vegas. In the mid-'50s, he formed the Sloan Company, which represented a number of film and stage stars (including Mae West, Marlene Dietrich, and Carol Channing, among others), as well as various corporations and trade associations.